# ANYTHING IS POSSIBLE

10 Keys to Unlock the Life of Your Dreams

**SADIE KOLVES**

*Anything is Possible: 10 Keys to Unlock the Life of Your Dreams*

© 2020 Sadie Kolves

All rights reserved. No portion of this book may be reproduced, stored in a retrieval system, or transmitted in any form or by any means—electronic, mechanical, photocopy, recording, scanning, or other—except for brief quotations in critical reviews or articles, without the prior written permission of the publisher.

Printed in the United States of America.

ISBN 9781735391106 paperback

ISBN 9781735391113 ebook

Cover Design by: Kristi Griffith, GoThumbprint.com

Cover Photo by: Boy Aaron Photography, BoyAaronPhotography.com

*Dedicated to Brent, for being there every step of the way, and Savannah, for being patient with me and inspiring me to become my best self.*

# CONTENTS

| | |
|---|---|
| Introduction | vii |
| 1. Embrace Your Destiny | 1 |
| 2. Believe in Yourself | 17 |
| 3. Find Your Why | 34 |
| 4. Learn From Your Failures | 48 |
| 5. Focus on the Future | 62 |
| 6. Practice Consistent Habits | 76 |
| 7. Choose Your Friends Wisely | 90 |
| 8. Take Care of Your Body | 107 |
| 9. Live Debt-Free | 124 |
| 10. Give Generously | 141 |
| Acknowledgments | 155 |
| About the Author | 157 |

# INTRODUCTION

One morning in the Spring of 2010, I woke up, looked in the mirror, and didn't recognize the person staring back at me.

It had been nearly a year and a half since my father had a massive brain stroke at the age of fifty-six. It was December 18, 2008—a date that is etched in my memory. He died a few days later on December 22, the day before Christmas Eve.

I was broken and lost. All the hard work I had done to hold my family together as a single mother was gone in an instant. I was weak and began slipping into a deep depression. To help me sleep, I went back to smoking pot (an old habit from my younger days). Some weekends, I would go out drinking with the girls. I just wanted to escape reality and check out of life for a while.

That was only the latest in a long string of setbacks and disappointments. In my thirty years of life, I'd been abandoned, abused, neglected, incarcerated, addicted, foreclosed on, cheated on, and lied to.

And on top of all that, I had gained twenty pounds!

I stood there looking at the stranger in the mirror, and one word dominated my mind.

*Enough.*

In a moment of decision, I stormed to the kitchen and began tossing out all the processed food and sugary snacks. I grabbed a trash bag and went through the refrigerator, freezer, cabinets, and every drawer.

I completely changed my life. I started eating healthier and working out. This went on for months until one day I realized I had dropped all my extra weight. It felt like it happened overnight, but of course, that wasn't true. After keeping my head down and working so hard, it sure felt that way.

That was the moment I realized that if you stick to one thing long enough, you *will* have success. I knew that *anything was possible.*

What about you? Do *you* believe anything is possible?

If you answered *yes* to that question, you're in the right place. You probably have a positive outlook on life, and you're hoping to learn a few tips to take your life to the next level. You'll find a lot of strategies and practical suggestions here.

If you answered *no*, you're *especially* in the right place. Maybe life has beaten you down to the point where you have lost hope. Maybe you have recently lost a job, you're on the edge of financial disaster, or your marriage is on the rocks. Maybe you've given up hope and you're staring into the pit of despair, wondering if there is any reason to go on.

I can relate. As you'll see in the coming chapters, there have been times in my life that were as dark and hopeless as anything you'll see on a bad TV movie at three in the morning. But in the span of only a few short years, I found true love, got in the best shape of my life, and built a multiple six-figure business.

I want success for you, too, which brings me to the reason why I wrote this book—to share what I've learned on the journey to building the life of my dreams.

Most people think success is a great mystery. They don't understand why some people thrive, while others struggle. They believe life is a great big lottery where people are either lucky or unlucky.

Don't believe it for one minute. Success isn't a mystery. As Earl Nightingale once said, "Success is the progressive realization of a worthy goal." All it takes is some know-how and the willingness to be consistent in the right actions.

You can unlock the life of your dreams if you are willing to do the work. I wrote this book to share the ten most important keys to unlocking your dream life. No matter who you are or where you're from, I'm thrilled to share this journey with you.

Before we go any further, let me share a few suggestions to help you get the most out of this book:

First, skip around as needed. The chapters follow a logical sequence, but each one also stands on its own.

Second, use the suggestions in the "Unlock the Possibilities" section at the end of each chapter to help you apply the principles you're learning.

Third, take action. Don't wait until life is perfect, or you have everything figured out. Imperfect action beats perfect inaction every time!

My story is your story. We may have different backgrounds, but there is one thing we have in common: we all have scars. If I can rise from the ashes like a phoenix, you can, too!

I'm so glad you're here. There are a million other books you could read, but you chose mine. I'm grateful for the chance to help you discover that anything is possible.

Love,
Sadie

## 1. EMBRACE YOUR DESTINY

Remember the classic 1980s movie *Back to the Future?* The one with the time-traveling DeLorean, crazy Doc Brown, and Marty McFly stuck in 1955?

Marty has two goals: 1. Help his future parents George and Lorraine fall in love. 2. Get back to 1985. If he doesn't accomplish the first one, he and future siblings will be erased from existence . . . and getting back to 1985 won't matter.

A great scene in the middle of the movie sums up the whole story. With Marty's help, George finally works up the nerve to tell Lorraine how he feels about her. He goes to the local diner, approaches her table, and stammers for a bit.

Then he utters the classic line, "I'm George. George McFly. I'm your *density* . . . I mean, your *destiny*."

Lorraine is intrigued, and George is relieved that it's finally off his chest. Just then, the town bully, Biff, storms into the diner looking for George. Fortunately, Marty saves the day and keeps Biff from beating up George. But unfortunately, Lorraine is now even more in love with Marty.

It's the classic situation—one step forward, two steps back. Just when George's "destiny" seemed within reach, life threw a monkey wrench into his plans.

Have you ever felt like George McFly, as if the universe is conspiring against you? Like your destiny is just out of reach?

If so, I can relate.

## MY STORY

I grew up in a family that didn't believe we were destined for success. We were poor, and in our family, a woman's destiny was to get married and have babies. If she was lucky, she might have a job at some point. College was out of the question.

My mom had four kids by the time she was twenty. In addition to my twin sister and me (we were born in 1980), I had an older brother and sister. My earliest memories of my family are happy, except for the usual family hijinks like my brother busting my lip open with a Tonka truck when I was four.

For the first few years, life was normal. But it was not to last.

My mother was a stay-at-home mom. In 1985, she decided she wanted to have an identity outside the home, so she started teaching aerobics. That was the beginning of the end of our little family as I knew it. She was spending a lot of money on clothes, which was a problem since my dad didn't make much money. (In fact, we only had one family car.)

Dad worked a lot, so we didn't spend a lot of time with him. I was a momma's girl. However, this bond was strained as she became more distant. One time, I hid in the back seat of the car when she was headed to aerobics so I could spend time with her. I got into trouble, as you can imagine.

Another time, my twin sister and I got into Mom's makeup. She was very upset and locked us out of the house in the middle of a thunderstorm. She refused to let us back in, even though we were just five years old.

Things went downhill, and Dad tried to save their marriage through counseling, but she wouldn't go. One time, he planned a romantic evening, complete with candles, but she got upset and ruined it all. I remember the yelling. There was so much yelling.

In 1986, Mom left my Dad and took me and my two sisters to our great-grandmothers and my brother to my grandmother's. She didn't tell my dad where we were for the whole summer. She left all of us kids there and stayed with her boyfriend. Dad found out where we were and came to get us. That's when we found out he only had twenty percent of his kidney function left.

Mom filed for divorce in 1987, at the same time my dad was going through kidney failure and lost his job. He didn't want to deal with us kids, so he gave custody to her, but she didn't want it. Neither parent wanted the hassle of dealing with four children.

In the end, we stayed with our dad. Later that year, his kidneys failed, and he started dialysis. He had to apply for public aid and food stamps and got on the transplant list. He was a bitter and broken man who blamed us kids for Mom leaving.

At that point, my mom wouldn't see us. On the weekends we were supposed to go see her, she wouldn't show up. We would wait by the window watching for the car, and after the sun went down, we would watch for a car blinker, hoping she would come. The few times she did show up, she had her boyfriend's son with her, which was disappointing because she was spending time with another kid. That went on for about a year.

We were "Momma's girls," so when she left, we were broken and confused. We found a white coat that smelled like her. My sister and I would sleep with it, each holding an arm.

From my vantage point as a kid, all I could see were the same patterns and dysfunctions repeating themselves. My dad would say, "You are where you're from." In his mind, our destiny was set. He believed we didn't have any choice in the matter. He would also say, "We don't come from money, like so-and-so. They got lucky. We're not going to have that kind of money."

It never occurred to me as a kid that we could change our destiny—that we could have something more. I didn't think I deserved to be successful. I never imagined I could have different or better opportunities.

Maybe this is how you grew up as well. Maybe you have this mindset right now. Maybe you feel like George McFly through most of *Back to the Future*—your destiny awaits, then awaits some more, like it's always just out of reach.

No matter what your background is, or how you grew up, or what your situation is right now, I'm here to tell you that success *is* possible. I believe your destiny is to be successful, and I want you to believe it, too.

But you have to do more than believe that success is possible. You have to embrace this truth with every part of your being. You have to stop limiting your beliefs about what is possible.

How do you do this? You do it by figuring out what success means for you, and then believing that you deserve it.

## DEFINING SUCCESS

If you could take a poll of one hundred people right now, how many would say they want to be successful?

You guessed it. Probably every one of them!

Now, what if you asked each of those people how they define success in specific terms. Only a small percentage would be able to tell you in concrete terms what success means to them.

Everyone wants to be successful, but almost no one

takes the time to figure out what that means. You can't embrace your destiny as a successful person unless you first define what it means.

My definition of success has changed over time. As a kid, it was going to school and coming home to cook dinner for my dad without being yelled at. As a teenager, it was making it through the day. As an early adult, it was raising my daughter. But now, at this stage of my life, I define success by my mental happiness and the happiness of my family. Success also means financial freedom and crushing every single goal that I have.

It wasn't always this way. There was a time when all I cared about was being the best mom I could be and paying the bills. But as my life changed, my idea of success changed along with it.

As I'm writing this, my idea of success includes growing my business, staying healthy, and helping my daughter find a good college. I'm thrilled to be living a life that I couldn't even have imagined only a few years ago.

Take a few minutes to figure out what success means for you. Write it down somewhere that you will see it often.

All done? Good! (Don't continue reading until you've written it down.)

Now that you've figured out your definition of success, you need to accept and believe that you deserve it. That's hard for many people because they were raised to believe they would never be successful. It was the case for me.

If that is how you grew up, you have some work to do. It takes time and emotional energy to get past the negative thinking of the people who influenced you as a kid. But believe me, it's worth it!

When I was younger, I would ask, "Why do I deserve success?" Now I ask the opposite question. "Why *don't* I deserve success?"

God put us on this earth for a purpose, and it's bigger than we can ever imagine. We all deserve success in every aspect of our lives. We all deserve to live a life of happiness.

It's not only about us as individuals. We're all here to help other people have better lives—not just our children but also our friends, neighbors, clients, customers, community, and ultimately, the world.

What is your idea of happiness? My idea of happiness is having the freedom to travel and see the world because we're here for such a short time. We all deserve that. We all deserve to see what God created. We shouldn't be confined to just one place on this spectacular planet.

We are all worthy of success, but many people make excuses for why they're not successful. You must not only define success and then believe you deserve it. You must also take action.

If you want to make more money while sitting on the couch and watching Netflix all day, it's probably not going to happen. If you want to lose weight while eating

McDonald's every day, it's probably not going to happen. I could give other examples, but you get the point. You have to take action toward those dreams. You deserve it, and you are worthy, but you still have to work for it.

In the rest of this chapter, we'll walk through five habits that will help you take action and embrace your destiny as a successful person. These are not necessarily the typical "success habits" you read about all the time. But let's be honest; a lot of the typical advice doesn't work. These habits have helped me keep my sanity and survive and thrive in my life and business. I know they will help you, too.

## HABIT #1: KNOW YOUR WEAKNESSES

Imagine that you are taking a trip across a big city. Shortly after you leave, your phone alerts you that there is road construction ahead. If you stay on this route, you will face major delays because of traffic.

Would you continue the same way, or would you take another route?

The answer is simple; you would take a different route. But a simple solution when it comes to traffic is not such a simple solution when it comes to other areas of our life. We often keep going in the same direction even though we know there will be major problems!

Sometimes, life is sending us major "construction ahead" warning signs, but we choose to ignore them because we don't want to admit there is a problem.

On your journey to embracing your destiny of success, you will encounter weaknesses and roadblocks. You are likely already aware of your major flaws. But the question is, what are you going to do about them?

That's where self-knowledge comes in. If you don't know yourself well enough to deal with your weaknesses, it will be hard to reach your true potential.

My health and energy are important to me. I work out almost every day. But here's a little secret; I don't always feel like doing it. On those days when I don't feel like getting up, I remind myself that I'm weak right now. Knowing that about myself helps me get up and start moving. Once I'm walking, I'll eventually begin running because I start to feel it.

Maybe you feel weak in a different area, such as eating well, controlling your temper, getting work done, or saving money. Whatever it is, admit that you are weak. Write it down and say it out loud. It may feel a little silly at first, but it's a powerful way to take control of your weaknesses.

We all have weaknesses. That's okay. It means we're human. Don't try to tackle everything at once. Just take it one area at a time. If you try to lose a hundred pounds in one week, you're going to fail hard. Shoot for a smaller goal you can achieve.

We live so much of our lives driven by emotion. If you let emotions run your life, you get into trouble. When you feel weak and want to give up, take action immediately to do the right thing. Every time you do that, you get a little stronger.

## HABIT #2: FIGHT YOUR OWN DEMONS

That probably seems like a strange habit. You may be thinking, "Sadie, I thought this was a book about success. Why are you talking about demons?"

Well, the truth is that everybody has a little devil on their shoulder. Every time you have the impulse to do something good, that little devil is right there with you, whispering in your ear. "You don't want to go out and exercise today." "You don't want to go for that job interview." "You don't want to eat healthy today."

He's not only trying to keep us from doing good things; he also whispers lies into your ear. "You'll never be thin." "You don't measure up." "You're not as talented as she is."

You know the demon is there. But what can you do about it?

If you're waiting on someone to motivate you or move you, then the victory will never be yours. Each person has to decide to fight their own demons. It's hard because you're never fighting on your own ground. You have to go where the demons exist and fight them there.

Where do they exist? In your mind. That's both good news and bad news.

First, the bad news. Your demons are always with you. Because they exist in your mind, you can never escape them. Remember that Saturday Night Live sketch from the 1990s where Chris Farley played a motivational speaker? At one point in the sketch, he tells David Spade how he's going to be right by his side. "Here's you, here's Matt! Here's you, here's Matt!"

Demons are like that. Wherever you go, they go, too.

But here's the good news. You can fight the demons on their turf, which is your mind. You have control over your mind, so you have a lot of say about what goes on there, including how much power the demons have over you.

One of the recurring themes you'll hear me talk about in this book is the power of your mindset. Mindset literally means, "How you set your mind." Without a proper mindset, all is lost. We'll keep coming back to this theme over and over again.

I didn't say it was easy. But it's possible. You have to develop the spirit of a fighter. Are you ready to rumble?

## HABIT #3: WRITE DOWN YOUR GOALS

Most people believe that achieving your goals is a big complicated process. But I'm here to tell you that it doesn't have to be complicated. It's quite simple.

It's a pretty straightforward process to make your dreams a reality. You pick a goal that's important to you, and then you consistently work toward that goal.

But here's where most people get tripped up; they don't write down their goals. If you get nothing else out of this chapter, please remember this one piece of advice.

When you write down your goals and then look at them every day, it affects your brain. It imprints the goal in your mind and starts to impact your behavior.

Let's say you want to start waking up earlier. You'd start by writing down your goal on a small piece of paper and then posting it where you can see it several times each day (for example, your bathroom mirror). But don't just write something like "Goal: Wake up earlier." Instead, write it as if you are already living your goal. "I am a person who wakes up early."

Most of the time, we stay stuck where we are because we don't take the actions to move forward. But when you write down your goals as if you're already achieving them, and then post them where you can see them, your actions will start to conform to the goals. It's almost as if you are speaking that goal to yourself over and over again. That little piece of paper is like a powerful magnet that is pulling you toward success!

## HABIT #4: MEDITATE

One of the hardest things about living in our modern, super-connected world is that we are constantly distracted.

Even if you know your weaknesses, fight your demons, and write down your goals, you're still going to deal with hundreds of daily distractions that can knock you off course.

Consider all the inputs you deal with on any given day: text messages, emails, commercials, websites, advertisements, and interruptions of every kind. It never ends. It's enough to drive you crazy!

That's why I'm a true believer in meditation. I know, I know . . . many people think meditation is some kind of "woo-woo" magic that isn't real. But it's made a huge difference in my life. If you study the habits of the world's most successful people, meditation is one of the most common practices you will find.

There are many types of meditation, but the basic idea is to slow down and give your mind and heart a break. When you meditate, it's a rare moment to calm down and just *be*.

Squirrel! That's what I'm like much of the time. I'm constantly distracted, and it's hard for me to stay focused. When I meditate, I find a quiet place and try to clear my mind. Then I focus on my breathing, which helps me keep my mind clear.

It's easy to get distracted when you meditate. That's okay. Let your thoughts come and go as they please. The more you *try* to focus, the harder it will be. The whole point of meditation is letting go and calming down. Guided meditation can also be very helpful, whether through an in-person coach, audio, or a meditation app like Headspace or Calm.

In your quest to step into your destiny, don't be so focused on the end result that you get burned out. Meditation is a great way to take care of your mind and body, so you have the focus and energy to stay in it for the long haul.

## HABIT #5: STOP SETTLING

Let me share one final habit before we begin winding down this chapter. It's a habit that's easy to overlook if you're not careful.

Think about your grade school history class for a moment. Remember what they called the people who were the first to arrive in a new land? They were called "settlers." Today, we don't have many "settlers of the land" because most of the Earth has been explored. But we have many "settlers of the heart."

These are people who have settled for less than they want in life. They want something more, but the pain involved in being more successful is too great to bear.

This question is uncomfortable, but try to answer it honestly. Are you settling?

If the answer is yes, I want you to know that the pain and struggle are worth it. When you decide to stop settling, you will lose friends and family who can't handle your success. That's what happened to me. When I changed my life, I began to lose a lot of friends. They didn't like the fact that I wasn't content to be a settler anymore.

You get one shot at life, and you can't live it for somebody else. There is no reason to be miserable if you can have more happiness and success.

In my business, we work with many women whose husbands are not supportive. These women want to achieve more for themselves and their families, but the husbands aren't on board. That presents a difficult choice.

Everyone's situation is different, but I do know this; if you don't have the support of the people in your life, it's much harder to be successful. Sometimes you have to make the difficult choice to cut ties and move on.

You only get one shot at this life. Don't you owe it to yourself to make the most of it?

## YOU'RE MEANT FOR THIS

I opened this chapter with a reference to *Back to the Future*. George McFly found his *destiny* when he won over Lorraine, his future wife. If he hadn't done that, it would have put Marty's entire existence in jeopardy.

George's destiny wasn't just about him. It was also about his whole family. As we discovered in the sequels, *Back to the Future Parts II & III*, small changes in the present can make a difference for the future, either for good or bad.

Your destiny is not only about you; it's also about those you love. If you're married, it's also about your spouse. If you're a parent, it's also about your kids. Ultimately, it's also about your friends, clients, business partners, and anyone else you come in contact with.

It sounds intimidating, but don't let it scare you. You can do this! You're *meant* for this. There is nothing more satisfying than becoming the person you're meant to be.

## UNLOCK THE POSSIBILITIES

To begin embracing your destiny:

1. Write down what success means for you. Be as specific as possible.

2. Pick a goal you want to achieve or a habit you want to change in the next six weeks. Get a piece of paper *right now*, write it down, and tape it to your bathroom mirror, so you see it every morning.

3. In the next twenty-four hours, take five minutes to meditate. If you've never done it before, give it a shot. You will be surprised at the benefit you will get from a simple five minutes of meditation.

## 2. BELIEVE IN YOURSELF

*I don't want to be divorced.*

Those were the words going through my mind as I mentally ticked off my list of options. The list consisted of exactly two items: 1) Stay in an unhealthy marriage; or 2) Get a divorce.

Nobody enters into a marriage thinking they will be contemplating divorce someday—especially at twenty-eight years old. You get married believing and hoping for the best. But sometimes, the choice is made for you.

I wondered how things had gotten so far off track in the nine years Erik and I had been together. I was only nineteen years old, working at Walmart. That's where we first met, and I fell head over heels in love with him.

We dated for nine months, and Erik decided to join the Army. We planned to stay together, and then I would move with him. He left for basic training, and I wrote him a letter every single day. I didn't miss one day. He wrote a letter to ask my dad if he could marry me—all the things he thought you were supposed to do. We were going to get married on December 23, 1999. During that time, I decided to go back to school and get my high school diploma. I was *so* proud of myself.

I picked him up from the airport, assuming we would still have our wedding before celebrating Christmas together. His mom was *not okay* with the wedding, so he backed out. I was heartbroken.

Erik still wanted me to move to Hinesville, Georgia, once he finished AIT (Advanced Individual Training). He got out, moved himself to Georgia, and I followed one month later. His mom would have been livid if she had known. Erik was a *huge* momma's boy and never wanted to disappoint her. He didn't tell her I was coming. He said he still wanted to get married and that he had backed out because of his mom.

We were married in Ridgeland, South Carolina on March 30, 2000. I was so happy. But within two months, I was totally homesick. I missed my dad and worried that something would happen to him without me there. He had already been on dialysis for thirteen years.

I told Erik that I was going back, and he said he was miserable, too. He hated his job in the Army because he wasn't doing what he had signed up to do. So, we both packed up and simply left. He went AWOL (Absent Without Leave), and I was a big part of why. I was too young to understand what that meant or the penalties he would face.

His parents were so disappointed and upset with him. We ended up staying at my dad's house with our new dog for six months. Dad was still difficult to deal with. He complained that Erik was lazy and didn't do anything. Dad acted that way to anyone who lived with him.

I got a job at a bank, and Erik eventually got a job at a company that made washers. We found a townhouse in Belleville, Illinois, and life started looking good. His parents were willing to have me over for dinner like I finally existed. That was the first time I realized that all parents weren't like mine. Erik's mother was caring, kind, and always saying such positive things about him and his brother. She cooked meals, was an amazing wife, and had a nice house. I loved that she was my mother-in-law.

I began to believe in myself. I saw a different future for me. I was going to have the white picket fence with an awesome husband and amazing in-laws. She was like the mom I never had.

In October of 2001, I got a job as a receptionist. I felt important sitting at a big desk in a building made out of glass. I was twenty years old and doing just fine, making a whopping $18,500 per year. Erik started a job to learn carpentry and build homes.

I was still in training when the call came. It was one month after 9/11. Erik had been pulled over while he was on a lunch break, and there was a federal warrant for his arrest. Back to Georgia, he went to await trial. He came back a few times to visit while he was back in his Army routine. It was going to be six months before he stood trial. I had gotten called to testify, and I drove down with his mom. I was young, scared, and embarrassed. I got called to the stand, and I cried. I talked about my dad's illness and how it had led us to move so quickly, praying that the sad story would be enough.

Erik received the maximum sentence they requested —six months in the brig (military prison). We were back to writing letters every day. We thought they might give him an early release, but they didn't. They were keeping him in. It was going to be a process. I had to leave my job, pack up our home, and move back to Georgia. At least this time, we had support from his parents, and they helped us with this transition.

I handled it much better this time. I had a support system and a friend in his mom. She was someone I could call when I was down and needed someone to talk to. I'm not sure how I would have made it through that difficult time without her.

After Erik was released, we moved to Wentzville, Missouri. We were free and clear from the military and could finally get a fresh start. I got a job as a receptionist with a healthcare company, and Erik began working for the railroad. We were making more money than we ever had and were able to move to Florissant, Missouri. He began to work with a railroad tie gang, which required him to travel since it involved maintaining and repairing tracks.

Late that year, he became distant. We weren't talking as much when he was away. I noticed the cell phone bill was close to $300 for the second month in a row. The first month I thought maybe he had gone over the usage and didn't pay attention. The second time, I dug deeper. I took out the bill and looked hard at the numbers. There was a lot that seemed off. The next day at work, I decided to play detective and called the numbers. There were two; one was a hospital, and the other was the voicemail of a girl named Tiffany.

I called Erik to confront him. The girl was from Missouri, and he had gone to dinner with her a few times. I felt like I had been stabbed directly through my heart. I had never felt so broken in my life. I felt like I was going to be sick. I never thought he would do something like that. I thought we had the best, solid relationship, and so did our family and friends.

That day, he came home shortly after I did. I ran out to the car and punched him twice in the face. I showed zero mercy. I was so sad and broken, and he was *so* sorry. I called his mom the next day, and she didn't believe it was true. She asked how I knew, and I said he had told me. She said, "You can't get a divorce." I didn't want a divorce because I loved him. Months went by, and we gradually healed. Our relationship became solid again . . . or at least I thought.

## DESCENDING INTO CHAOS

I began applying for jobs in Illinois and got a job at a cancer treatment center. We decided to move closer to my dad and built a home in Lebanon, Illinois. I finally decided it was time to become a mom after five years of marriage.

It was an amazing pregnancy. I don't think it could have been any better. I had Savannah on March 16, 2006, the best day of our lives. I'd had a C-section, so I was able to enjoy twelve weeks off from work. I loved being a mom.

Erik was still traveling for his job. Around October 2006, he began drifting. He seemed distant, and our relationship quickly changed. His parents moved in with us because they decided to move back to Illinois to be closer to their grandkids. His whole demeanor was changing rapidly, and things got so bad that his parents moved out. Erik wouldn't even watch Savannah while I worked. I would still take her to daycare during my three workdays each week, so that he could relax at home for eight days.

Once again, I dove into the phone bill to see what I could find. I also hacked into his social media accounts. I discovered that he was talking to multiple girls. And not just a couple—it was in the double digits. I made phone calls and found messages. It was worse than I imagined. No wonder he withdrew from his family and became distant.

I lived like that for a year and a half. He left our family and moved in with his mom in April of 2008. He left me with $50,000 in credit card debt and a mortgage. Then our house went into foreclosure, and I lost my car.

I did not want to be divorced. I was the only one of

my siblings still married, and I wanted to keep it that way. But as I said, sometimes the choice is made for you. I felt like everyone in my life assumed I would be like my mom (who left my dad when I was a kid) or my sister (who was divorced). I didn't want to be compared to them.

I felt like a complete failure. I was all alone, left to care for my young daughter, as I struggled to make sense of the situation. If I didn't believe in myself, there was no way I was going to get out of this situation. It was do or die.

I put my focus on my daughter, my health, and my job. I was so focused on those three things that I didn't have time for anything else. As we will talk about later in the book, fitness impacts every area of your life. When I was in the middle of this dark situation, fitness gave me energy and hope. It boosted my confidence and helped me put one foot in front of the other every single day.

I wasn't doing this only for me. I was doing it for my daughter. My mom left when I was a kid, and I wanted to be the mom that I never had. But I had to believe in myself first.

But how do you develop a belief in yourself? How do you know if you can pull it off? And what happens when you truly believe in yourself? Those are some of the questions we'll explore in this chapter.

Here's what I know; nobody's going to do it for you. Even if you have the world's best support network, there comes a time when you must stand on your own and start believing in yourself. When you do, you'll be amazed at how it impacts your life and everyone around you.

The real question is, where do you start?

## GETTING STARTED

Most people live with a mix of confidence and doubt. Nobody is confident a hundred percent of the time. Likewise, it's rare to find someone who has no self-confidence at all.

But there are times in your life when you're going through a bad patch, and you have no idea how you'll make it through. The walls are closing in and you can't find the strength to keep going.

I've been in this situation before, and here's what I have learned—you start by consistently making time for yourself. To all the Moms reading this, we are especially prone to putting ourselves last. We feel guilty if we are not available for our husband or kids 24/7. But if you're not making a little time for yourself, you're depleting yourself and not bringing your best to your family.

It's vital to take a little time every day for self-care. You're worth every minute of it. I don't care of it's just fifteen or twenty minutes a day. The time you spend on self-care will make a huge difference in your mental and emotional state.

It's also important to get on a schedule. One of the best things you can do for yourself is to get fit. Exercising at the same time each day is important because it establishes a habit. The more you do it, the easier it gets.

The same is true for personal development. Let's say you take 8:00-8:30 p.m. each night for yourself, or whenever works best for you. When you have already established that time, you can look forward to it without feeling guilty because you've already built it into your day. And since you've decided it ahead of time, you don't have to search for a chunk of time during the day. It's already planned.

Whether it's exercise, personal development, or some other activity that improves your mood and attitude, you'll start to feel better when you are consistent. As you build momentum, you can see what works for you and make adjustments to include more of that in your life.

When everything in your life is out of whack, the first place to start is by getting on a consistent schedule. If you're a parent, you know that getting a young child off their schedule creates a lot of problems. They get irritable and out of sorts. The same thing happens to us!

When you stay up too late, sleep too late, and don't have any structure in your life, you get cranky and irritable, just like your kids. When things are going badly, get back on a schedule.

Here's one thing I wish I would have told myself years ago: it's essential to do things that make you happy. We get stuck in the routines of being a parent or grandparent and forget where our true happiness lies.

What brings you joy?

I love working in the garden, but I haven't done that since we lived in New Mexico. We did a little bit of gardening after we first moved here, but we don't have much of a yard. I miss that because it's a release for me. I love getting my hands dirty and working with potted plants.

I also love going to events and meeting new people. It's so important to make connections with people who share your interests. When you love what they love, you can support each other and build new relationships that help you be more successful. Great friends make a world of difference when life is spinning out of control.

When you're lost, go back to those activities that give you joy. Go back to the basics and focus on the simple things that make you happy.

It's easy to overcomplicate things, especially if you're an analytical person. But you just need to get started. Don't overthink things. You'll find your confidence when you take small actions like giving yourself some "me" time and going back to the simple things that bring you joy.

## CAN WE DO THIS?

One of the most fascinating periods in U.S. history is the 1960s. Not only do you have massive social upheaval and the Vietnam War, but you also have the fascinating story of NASA's missions to the moon.

One of the overriding questions NASA faced was, "Can we do this?" Was it possible to develop the technology, processes, and infrastructure to take a crew to the moon and return them safely to Earth?

Despite all the unknown factors and the enormous cost of the 1960s space program, NASA forged ahead and eventually achieved its mission. But the question "Can we do this?" was never fully resolved until Neil Armstrong set foot on the moon in 1969.

You have goals you want to accomplish. There are obstacles in your way. You're wondering if it's possible. Is your goal or objective realistic, or are you living in a fantasy world?

The question is staring you right in the face. *Can you actually do this?*

If you want to live a bigger life, that question never goes away. As soon as you accomplish one goal, you'll develop another one, and that question of possibility will raise its head again.

I believe anything is possible. And I believe that if you work hard enough, you can accomplish anything if you never give up. However, it also depends on whether your goals are realistic. For example, if you want to play for the NBA but you're a 5'6" guy who is forty-five years old and has never worked out, that's probably not going to happen.

There is an element of being realistic about your goal. You need to understand what is within the realm of possibility. That is where it's helpful to have great friends who can give you a fair assessment of reality. Does your goal have limitations? If you're that 5' 6" guy and want to play for the NBA, you have limitations you can't overcome.

When you talk about doing something like starting a business, anyone can do that. Even if you have no money or experience, those are limiting factors that you can overcome.

If your goal is based in reality and you're serious about it, it's vital to make a plan. A goal with no plan of action is nothing but a dream. You may not be able to play for the NBA, but you can become a *better* basketball player. And if that's what you want to do, what is your plan for making it happen?

Write it down. Get detailed. Create a plan for doing it. Be realistic, but also push yourself.

It's vital to have good friends who will help you. Yes, you must believe in yourself, but those friends will help you get a realistic view of your situation. Are they in the trenches with you? Or are they just giving you empty advice? Never take advice from someone who hasn't been where you want to go.

When you go after it, you'll soon find out if it's realistic or not. While you may or may not reach your ultimate goal, that's almost beside the point. The real issue is whether you did your best and grew as a person. Did you rise to your full potential? If so, you've achieved all you can do.

## IT'S NOT JUST ABOUT YOU

We may not know each other personally, but I know one thing about you: you're facing a challenge.

It might be a huge challenge like a health crisis, financial problems, a death in your family, or a divorce. Or it might be a smaller challenge that isn't going to wreck your life, but it's still something you must deal with.

You might be facing several major problems at once. If so, my heart goes out to you. I've been there, done that, and have the t-shirt to prove it.

But here's a truth that will give you hope. It's not only about you. When my husband left, I had to figure things out for myself. Besides my daughter and myself, I didn't give much thought to who else's life I might affect by choosing to press on. But come to find out, my brother said I was the reason he went back to college. He saw that I was making something of myself. Since we came from the same family, he knew that if I could do it, he could do it, too.

People are watching and listening to see how you respond to whatever life throws at you. You can have an impact far beyond yourself. Just as George Bailey discovered at the end of *It's a Wonderful Life*, each person's life touches so many others.

You may not think you're making a difference, especially if you're going through a tough time. But I guarantee that you're touching people right where you are.

Your words, your attitude, and your actions all make a huge difference. Most of the time, we don't even know it.

There is another sense in which it's not only about you. There is a quote attributed to Plato: "Be kind, for everyone you meet is fighting a hard battle." Every time you interact with someone, you can be sure they are going through something hard. The more you believe in yourself and invest in your future, the more you can make a positive change in their life.

Hang in there and keep your chin up. If you don't believe in yourself and keep pressing on, it will leave an awfully big hole in the world.

## THE KEY WORD: BELIEF

At this point in the book, you've heard my story. You know that I had a difficult childhood and overcame many obstacles on my way to getting healthy, crushing my goals, and building a successful business.

When you believe in yourself, sometimes there will be people who talk bad about you. They'll try to tear you down because they can't stand it when someone tries to make something of their life. Remember that misery loves company. Just put your blinders on. Success and true happiness come as soon as you realize what others think about you is none of your business.

How do *you* think about you? That is the only thing that matters. People told me I wasn't good enough. They made me believe that a mediocre life was the best I could hope for. That's not exactly what you'd call an inspiring dream.

That's how we were raised. My grandfather never made more than two dollars an hour. He saved every penny. My grandparents never even traveled to the Ozarks of Missouri, and they lived just a few hours away. My family didn't travel. They stayed in the same small town their entire lives. I grew up believing that my main objective in life was to stay close to my family and help them, no matter what.

Let me tell you this. If someone is draining the life out of you and they are family, it is okay to step back and re-assess. You cannot be surrounded by those types of people and still grow. Once I met my first husband's parents, I learned that other types of families existed. They showed me that I *can* have a better life. I can travel, have a nice house, have nice things, and even have a good job.

I learned that I don't have to share my family's political views. I don't have to give my family money because they decided to make poor choices. I can live a great life, have my own opinions, and make my own choices without listening to someone complain that their way is the only way.

People lived differently, and I had no idea. That allowed me to dream. That was the moment in my life when I took immediate action and grew as a person. I fell in love with who I had become. I was so proud, and I worked really, really hard.

A lot of people tell themselves that they can never make a great living. They believe it can only happen to other people. I didn't graduate from college, so there is no way I could make good money, right? My dad told me I would never amount to anything. My teachers said I would be poor if I didn't graduate high school or go to college.

Do you know what they didn't teach at school (unless I missed that lesson)? Do you know what I didn't learn at home? I am capable of anything I put my mind to. I *can* make any income if I work hard and believe in myself!

The keyword is *belief*. Yes, hard work is a huge part of it. You need to be working when others are sleeping or watching TV. You often have to work when others are on vacation, having drinks, or sleeping in. You get my point. You have to *believe* in yourself.

Once I saw that my consistent actions were paying off, and everything was coming together, I began to believe it. Then *bam*! I was making over six figures a year. That was my goal growing up. Man, if I could make six figures, I would live a life I could enjoy.

Well, my belief has turned into a whole lot more than I ever imagined!

Listen, you can have anything you put your mind to. It doesn't mean it will happen this year or even next year. But if you work hard enough, and believe you will have it, you *will*. Don't compare your race to someone else's. You can't win someone else's race!

*I don't want to be divorced.* That's what I told myself

during one of the bleakest times of my life. But I chose to believe in myself. And because I did, I learned that anything is possible if you believe in yourself.

## UNLOCK THE POSSIBILITIES

To increase your self-confidence:

1. Pay attention to your self-care. What brings you joy? Write down three things you can do this week to lift your spirits and build your joy and confidence. When will you do them? (Be specific.)

2. What is the one big goal you'd like to accomplish in the next three years? Is it realistic? Be honest. Ask a trusted friend to give you feedback.

3. Write down the name of ten people whose lives you could impact if you believe in yourself 100% and work hard toward your goals.

# 3. FIND YOUR WHY

Imagine that you and your family are preparing for the vacation of your dreams. The car is packed, everyone is ready to go, and you've finalized all your plans. You slip into the driver's seat, ready for the adventure that lies ahead.

You insert the key into the ignition and turn it. Nothing.

"Hmm . . . that's strange," you wonder. "Maybe I need to check the battery." You turn the key again. Still nothing.

Frustrated, you pop the hood and get out of the car. When you fully open the hood to find the problem, you're baffled at the sight before you.

There's no engine!

That seems like a crazy scenario. Who would ever attempt to go on a long journey without an engine in the car? Yet that is the very situation many people encounter when they embark on a journey to embrace their destiny and achieve more than they ever dreamed.

Your *why* is the engine in the vehicle of your life. It's the reason you do what you do. It's what drives you to work hard, rise above the noise, and create a better life for you and your family.

Without a clear *why*, your life will stall out, and you'll be stuck.

But how do you find your why? How do you get clarity on your purpose? That's what we're going to explore in this chapter. I'm going to share five practices that have helped me discover my purpose, and I know they'll help you as well.

One thing before we dive in. You don't discover your purpose right away. The whole thing won't be clear all at once. It's a process. Every day that you follow these principles, your purpose and your big *why* will become clearer.

Ready to dive in?

## 1. LEARN TO LOVE MONDAYS

That might seem like strange advice. "Sadie, you're seriously telling me I should love Mondays? Mondays are the *worst* day of the week!"

Yep, I know it sounds weird. But hang with me for a second.

Most people hate Mondays because that's the day of the week that represents a job they hate. The weekend is over, and they have to slog back to five days of misery.

But that's the problem. Monday is not a day to dread. It's a day to *embrace*. Monday represents a brand-new start. No matter how bad last week was, you always get a fresh start on Monday.

Mondays are like big erasers. Whenever you use a dry-erase board, you can take that eraser and get rid of what you wrote.

Mondays work just like that. You can't wipe away the consequences of your actions, but you *can* get a brand-new start. Mondays are like a spring day with brand new buds blooming into flowers. It's beautiful in every way.

If you screwed something up, if you didn't eat right, if you didn't close a business deal, or something else went wrong . . . Monday is a fresh start. It's a new week. It's a chance to begin again. That's why it's my favorite day!

A lot of people say, "You can start any day. What's so special about Monday?" And they're right. You can have a fresh start any day of the week. But we tend to think in weeks. Those are the time blocks we use to organize our lives. Even if the whole previous week (or month) was bad, Monday is a great day for a new beginning, since it's the first day of the workweek.

I started to love Mondays when I became my own boss. That's because I was in charge of my own schedule. I didn't have a boss breathing down my neck, making every decision for me.

For most people, Mondays are the day when they feel

their freedom take a back seat to someone else's agenda (like their boss or company). But when you work for yourself, Monday is the day of the week when you get to dive back into work that you love!

When you find something you are passionate about, it doesn't feel like a job. It feels like fun. And when you're having more fun, you have more clarity about your why.

## 2. FIND JOY IN WHAT YOU'RE DOING

One of Bill Murray's most famous movies is *Groundhog Day*. He plays a reporter who keeps living the same day over and over again. His life is stuck in an endless loop.

Have you ever felt like that? Maybe you've gone for months (or even years or decades) feeling like you're repeating the same day over and over again. You wake up, go to a job you hate, come home, have dinner, go to bed, rinse, and repeat.

When your life is playing on an endless loop, how do you break the cycle and get unstuck? How do you start moving in a purposeful direction?

When I was working for someone else in a job I hated, I would tell myself one simple thing: "I don't want to wish my life away." So many people just want to get through the week so they can enjoy the weekend. When you hate Mondays because you're stuck in a job you don't like, you wish your life away.

It's important to find peace or some kind of joy in what you're doing. When you are working at a job you hate during the week, try to find something that you can do to bring you closer to your goals. Look for something fulfilling.

But how do you find fulfillment and joy in a job you hate? You have to flip the script. Instead of looking at Monday as a day to dread, look at it as a way to get ahead. It's an opportunity to learn a new skill, overcome challenges, and become stronger.

There are things you can do in any job that will help you move ahead. Even if you don't like your job, there are aspects of it that will apply to starting your own business. At the very least, it's another day you get to be alive.

Being in a job you hate also gives you direction about your future. Every job will help you understand your gifts and abilities better. It may not feel like it at the time, but you're always moving forward, even if it feels like you're stuck.

Does your job offer classes or training? Can you find a way to volunteer or take on a new project? Those are great opportunities to grow and learn right where you are.

It doesn't mean you have to stay there forever. You have opportunities for growth all around you. Even when you feel stuck, there is always something to learn that will help you in the future.

## 3. GET OUT OF THAT JOB YOU HATE

It may sound like I'm contradicting the last point, but I'm not. There are positive things you can learn from any job. But there comes a time when you have to escape from a job that does not help you reach your goals.

Let me tell you about one of the worst jobs I've ever had. I worked in the medical field, and all the negativity in that job began with the boss, which is where it usually starts and ends. If the boss is bad, it affects the whole place. If the problem is not the boss, but someone else, it's the boss's responsibility to fix it. So, either way, it comes down to the boss.

I had a female boss, and I would describe her as bipolar. She would be in a good mood one day and in a bad mood the next. (Women can be very moody and hard to work with. Just saying!) She would slam doors, and her unpredictable mood affected the whole workplace. I'm a happy and outgoing person, but it was making me miserable and taking away my joy.

But that's not all. There was a lot of down-time at that job. I would often think, *I could be doing something more productive with my time, like cutting my grass, planting flowers, or playing with my daughter.* I hated sitting in the office doing nothing.

I could outwork anybody. I could literally do three people's jobs in a day and still have down time. While I was there, I missed more important things in my life, like volunteering to read for my daughter's class at school. All

I wanted to do was be a mom. Working in this situation with a challenging boss was difficult.

After that boss was fired, we had a revolving door of interim bosses. One of them was a radiation oncologist manager who was filling in. He hit on me several times, and I always turned him down. When it came time for promotions, he turned the tables on me and never let me advance. Not only that, he also threatened to fire me twice.

I was working circles around other people. It's one thing to hit on someone, but it's another thing to threaten their job and keep them from advancing when they are more than qualified. I ended up going to the HR Department, and they did an investigation. During that time, I was advised to stay home for a week.

The boss ended up getting fired. In addition to the complaints I mentioned earlier, they discovered he was adding false information to people's files, among other ethical issues.

When I came back to work, the women treated me differently. You would have thought that I had made up some extravagant story about him. They treated me like I was the worst person on the planet. I thought to myself, *This is why women don't say anything when they are harassed. This is why women don't come forward.*

I shouldn't have felt horrible. I had every right to keep my job and work in a place where the boss did not hit on me and where I had a fair shot at promotions. That is often what corporate America is like.

I was miserable and knew that I was not making enough money for the work I was putting in, not to mention the hostile environment. I was missing out on my daughter's life. She was my big *why*.

After ten years in that environment, I moved on. I had to find my joy. I wanted to be able to live a different kind of life. I wanted to live on purpose, travel more, and be with my daughter.

That job, as bad as it was, was my jumping-off point for building a business. It gave me the motivation to take back control of my work and my life.

One day, I came home and said to my husband Brent, "Can we take a pay cut?" He said, "We'll make it work." We sacrificed and did not have a lot of money. We lived paycheck to paycheck for a while. We didn't travel or take on any unnecessary expenses. I put my head down, went to work, and started to create a life I never thought I would have.

It all started with getting out of a job that was making my life miserable.

## 4. START A BUSINESS

Most people can relate to my story of feeling stuck in a miserable job. Which begs the question, "Why then, do most of those people stay where they are? Why do most people choose to stay miserable rather than starting a business that will give them control over their life?"

Here's the reason. Starting a business feels intimidating to many people. But I can tell you from personal experience that when you start a business and do what it takes to be successful, you have a level of personal and financial freedom you can never imagine.

The only way you can live on your own terms is to have your own business. Otherwise, you will always be under someone else's control.

But where in the world do you start? Let me give you a few tips that will get you moving in the right direction.

The first thing you must do is get a mentor. You need to talk to somebody who is doing what you want to do. Find someone who is operating at the level where you envision yourself. If you want to make a million dollars, you're not going to talk to your cousin who lives in the trailer park . . . unless they also own the trailer park that's worth a million dollars!

When you find that person, ask them how they got started. Ask them what books they read, what courses they went through, and the steps they took to help build their business. It's all about developing the right mindset and taking action. It's not about intelligence and formal education. In fact, formal education often gets in the way of building a successful business. There are a lot of broke MBAs out there.

Success isn't complicated. It's quite simple. But the problem is that most people don't want to put in the work required to be successful. As they say, "Success leaves clues." All you need to do is follow the clues.

You also need to mentally prepare yourself for a lot of

setbacks. One of the most surprising aspects of starting a business is that people you would expect to support you will not do so. They don't want to support something they believe is going to fail. But secretly, they are too scared to do it themselves, so they don't support you.

That is an aspect of business that is hard for many people, especially if they can't handle rejection. But here's the thing: you may have a few people around you who are not supportive. But that doesn't compare to the hundreds or even thousands of people who are going to support and love you. Honest to God, you meet some of the best people by just following your dreams.

Those non-supportive people will see your success and then eventually notice. It's sad, but that's the way it is. Often, strangers will support you before your own family will. It's crazy but true.

It takes a long time to develop a powerful brand and build a solid list of clients or customers. Prepare for a long haul that consists of not just one war, but many little battles. It's not going to be a quick sprint. Building a business is a marathon.

But it's worth it! There's a lot more I could say on this topic, but here is the main thing: the only pathway to true freedom is having your own business.

## 5. STAY MOTIVATED THROUGH PERSONAL DEVELOPMENT

As you're building the life of your dreams, you will get tired. Not just physically, but emotionally and mentally as well. When you're tired, it's tempting to give up and quit too soon.

That's why it's crucial to stay motivated and work on your personal development. Every successful person, athlete, businessperson, CEO, and coach stays personally motivated. If you have a goal and want to achieve that goal, you have to motivate yourself.

There will be many mornings when you wake up and don't feel like doing something you promised yourself you would do. I never want to let someone else down, so it's easier to show up and be motivated when someone else is counting on you.

When it's for yourself, it's easy to let it slide since no one else knows but you. But that kills me. I will not let myself down. I have to live with the knowledge that I have disappointed myself. To stay motivated, I read great books and listen to podcasts.

After my first marriage ended, I moved into a tiny, asbestos-filled house. It was just my daughter and me. I had to motivate myself to be better and do better. Setbacks happened, but she depended on me (and I depended on me) to get my life together.

That's when I started paying attention to personal development. One of my favorite books was *Awaken the Giant Within* by Tony Robbins. I've listened to it three times (and it's a huge book!). It helped me become stronger and a better person overall.

I've seen Tony Robbins live, and I've never experienced anything like it. It was an event in Las Vegas, and I experienced every emotion I could possibly feel, yet it was intensified ten times over. It was amazing.

Other authors and leaders have influenced my life as well. Here are some of the books that have impacted me the most:

- *The Compound Effect* by Darren Hardy
- *The 10X Rule* by Grant Cardone
- *The Miracle Morning* by Hal Elrod
- *Atomic Habits* by James Clear
- *Can't Hurt Me* by David Goggins

These are a few that will get you started. No matter how successful you are, you need to stay motivated to improve your skills and mindset. You'll come up against the inevitable fear and doubt that will threaten to knock you off track.

I still deal with the fear of not accomplishing my goals. I still doubt myself and wonder whether I'm good enough. I still compare myself to others and wonder whether I'm as good as someone who seems to be faster or better.

Those are natural feelings everyone faces, no matter our level of success. We all need to listen and learn every day to keep moving ahead despite our doubt and fear.

I'm learning new things every single day. I will never reach a point in my life where I will know everything I need to know. The world is changing too fast, so if we want to stay current, we have to be constantly learning.

If you're struggling with your mindset, I encourage you to grab a book or listen to a podcast. Put in your earbuds and get started.

## PUTTING IT ALL TOGETHER

We have covered a lot of material in this chapter. But when you boil it all down, here is what it means: you have a purpose on this earth.

Some people are struggling, and they need to hear your message. They need to know how you have risen from the ashes and defeated your demons. They need to hear your inspiring story.

You also have a family who is depending on you. They need you to be at your best. They *deserve* your best.

It's all about finding your *why* and pursuing your purpose. But it's not just about you. *It's so much bigger than you.*

When you do work that makes you happy . . . when you take control over your life . . . when you stay motivated . . . when you have financial freedom . . . you are free to step into your God-given purpose.

And when that happens, you'll discover that *anything is possible*!

## UNLOCK THE POSSIBILITIES

To begin discovering your "why":

1. Answer this question honestly: Do you hate Mondays? What would it take for you to love Mondays?

2. If you are currently working at a job you don't like, what are three things about it that are helping you develop better skills?

3. Write down ten possible ideas for starting a business, then choose one that is easy, lucrative, and fun (ELF). What would it take to get started in that business in thirty days? Who is a person you know that is already having success in this type of business?

4. Choose one of the books I mentioned in this chapter and read it in the next thirty days.

## 4. LEARN FROM YOUR FAILURES

*Will she have the power to survive?*

That's the last line of the movie trailer for the 1984 movie, *Firestarter*. Drew Barrymore played a little girl with pyrokinesis (the ability to set things on fire with the mind). She's being pursued by a secret government agency, and the whole movie you are left wondering . . . *is she going to survive?*

That's a question you could have asked about me as a kid. Given the crazy environment where I was raised, I sometimes wondered that myself. Was I going to make it? How would this all turn out? Why was I going through all this?

It's no surprise that *Firestarter* was my favorite movie as a kid. Sometimes, I just wanted to burn it all down.

I don't think anyone would have blamed me. There I was, poor as dirt, living with a broken, verbally abusive father who never got over my mom leaving us. The only bright spot in the darkness was my grandmother (my dad's mother).

She was the only thing we had left after Mom left us. But when I was twelve, just getting ready to go into the seventh grade, we lost my grandmother. That was the summer I started dabbling in smoking. It was also the summer I got drunk for the very first time.

That was the beginning of the downward spiral.

Drugs and alcohol became my thing. I loved getting high. It was my escape from my reality. As long as I was high, I was happy. I never wanted to be home; I just wanted to escape.

I started using pot at age thirteen. When I was sixteen, I used crystal meth for the first time. It was truly an escape. I was so out of it that I started picking my face. I did this for so long that my boss asked if I had been into some magic mushrooms (I never used those). Meth started to become a normal thing for me, and then cocaine was introduced. On one occasion, I was up for more than three consecutive days. I must have looked awful as a five-foot-tall teen who weighed only eighty pounds.

I no longer lived at home. I was staying with a drug dealer and took advantage of the situation to get more drugs. That was my escape. I didn't want to participate in my life at home. I wanted a different life, and my drug-fueled environment provided exactly that.

One day, I was a passenger in a car, and my entire body began to feel paralyzed. I began to cry. I couldn't move my toes, fingers, or neck. I thought I was dying or having an overdose or withdrawal symptoms.

I have no idea what happened to me that day, but I was horrified. Of course, the driver wouldn't take me to the hospital because he was afraid. Instead, he took me back to his house and told me to lie down and that I should feel better. That entire time I swore to myself that I would never touch meth or cocaine ever again!

I stuck to that. One week later, I packed up my stuff and moved back in with my dad. I decided that I would apply for a full-time job since I had dropped out of high school a couple of years earlier, in 1996.

Maybe you have a similar story from your high school, college, or young adult years (or even right now). Maybe your story is completely different. Maybe your thing was never drugs or alcohol, but gambling, illicit sex, stealing, or some other secret.

I don't know you. But at the same time, I know you. We all have failures. We all have things that we wish were different about the past. We have all made mistakes and screwed up.

It's easy to become consumed with our past mistakes and the things we have done wrong. In the last chapter, we talked about finding your purpose—your *why*. But we can't do that until we begin to see our mistakes and failures in a different light.

We tend to look at failure as our enemy, as something to be avoided or swept under the rug. But failure is our best teacher. In the rest of this chapter, we'll look at five lies we believe about failure and why they're wrong.

## LIE #1: MY FAILURE DEFINES ME

There are moments in life when it seems you've hit rock bottom. You feel so low that you wonder if life is worth living anymore. Many people feel like failures because of their past or because of things going on in their lives. Social media only makes it worse since we constantly compare ourselves to others.

It's easy to think of yourself as a failure, as if that represents your total identity. But you're not a failure. You're a human being who is wonderfully and beautifully created in God's image.

You might have done things that failed. But you're never a failure.

If you're reading this, and today you feel like a total failure, I encourage you to talk to someone. You won't get through this on your own. If you are in danger of harming yourself, please call the National Suicide Prevention Hotline at 1-800-273-8255. Your health and safety are priority #1.

There was a point in my life when I wanted to die. I wasn't yet a teenager, but I seriously wondered if there was any point in going on with my life. Maybe you're in a similar place today. If so, you've got to talk to someone and realize that your mind is telling you the lie that you're a failure.

I also encourage you to find a church and talk to a counselor or pastor. The church represents the greatest hope we have, yet it's often the last place we turn to when it comes to finding solutions to our problems.

You are needed. You are wanted. You are loved. You matter. Do you honestly believe that your family and friends would be better off without you?

You have a purpose in this world. Maybe you're not feeling it right now, and maybe you have strayed away from it for a time. But the world needs you. Your family needs you.

Think of the simple conversations that have changed your life. What was the conversation that led to meeting your husband or wife? What was the conversation that led to the best job you ever had? What was the conversation that led to you meeting your best friend?

When you check out of life, you no longer have the ability to have those conversations. It's not just about you; it's about other people as well. If you're not here, you can't have those conversations that will help others.

Remember the movie *It's a Wonderful Life*? The main character, George Bailey, is having a terrible day and wishes he would have never been born. His wish is granted, and he gets to see what Bedford Falls would have been like without him.

It turns out that George had quite an impact on the people around him, and he never even knew it.

God put you on this earth to have an impact on other

people. But you have to get out of the mindset of feeling like a failure. You matter. You are enough.

## LIE #2: MY FAILURES HAVE TAKEN ME IN THE WRONG DIRECTION

There's an old saying, "Three steps forward, two steps back." That's what failure usually feels like.

If you've ever been hiking, you know that is not the case. When you go hiking, you take a winding trail through the wilderness. The trail goes up hills and down into valleys with plenty of switchbacks. You can walk for a while and wonder if you've made any progress at all.

Life is not a straight line from Point A to Point B. There are going to be all kinds of twists and turns in your story. The failures in your life are just switchbacks that are taking you through the winding trail of your life.

Failure means you are moving forward. If you're not failing, you're not growing and learning. The only person who doesn't fail is the one who sits motionless and doesn't attempt anything.

Do you feel like you're not a good enough wife? That you're not making enough money to support your family? That maybe you could be doing better in school? Maybe you feel like a failure as a parent because you can't pay for your kid's college.

Everybody feels like they are failing at something. The question is, what are you doing with that failure? Are you using it to your advantage?

The best thing you can do with failure is embrace it.

Failure is a learning experience that helps you do better. When you fail, just acknowledge that you need to work a little harder. You can figure out what you need to do to correct the issue or make the situation better.

Remember in the last chapter when I asked you to figure out your why and write down the steps to achieve it? Whenever you fail at something, that is a great time to revisit your why. Where did things go wrong? What can you change or do better?

No matter who you are or what you have achieved, there is always something you can do better. The trick is not taking failure personally. When you have fallen short, acknowledge the mistake, correct it, and move on. It's not a reflection of your value as a person. Failure is simply a measurement of your performance in a certain area. And there are always things you can do to improve your performance.

John Maxwell wrote a book called *Failing Forward*. That's a great title, isn't it? The next time you fail, remember to learn from the experience and fail forward.

## LIE #3: I'M DOING WORSE THAN EVERYONE ELSE

Imagine you are back in high school, taking an exam in math class. As you're taking the test, you realize you don't know all the answers. Everyone around you seems to be zipping through the test, getting all the answers right.

The bell rings at the end of class, and you give the test to the teacher. As you enter the hallway and start talking to the other students, you realize that everybody made mistakes on the test. Everyone else assumes they did worse than the others.

Life is like one big exam. When you're in the middle of it, things don't feel like they are going so well. But then, as you begin to talk to other people and learn how they are doing, you discover an important truth: nobody has it perfect. Everybody gets things wrong.

Look around at the people you know. Do some of them seem to have a perfect life? If so, think again. Everyone is making mistakes, and everyone has a boatload of failures you can't see.

For example, you've heard parts of my story so far in this book. But I'll bet you didn't know that I was once arrested and sent to jail as a teenager.

I didn't have a car because my dad had taken mine back. But I needed to run an errand, so I tried to take the car, but my sister Sarah wouldn't let me have it. We got into a big fight and she called the cops. While she was on the phone, I punched her in the back of the head. She and my brother both wrote a statement against me, so I was arrested and taken to the Clinton County jail.

I wasn't scared, but I was pretty mad that I couldn't get my hands on a cigarette. I was strip-searched and placed in an orange jumpsuit (just like the ones you see on TV). They put me in a holding cell with two large adult ladies. It was then that I realized I was really in jail.

One of the ladies was leaving for prison the next day. When I went to sleep, they stayed up playing cards, and the men in the cells next to us were yelling through the vents. I remember that I gave away my ham sandwich, and the vegetable soup had no flavor.

The next day, they shackled and chained me to a man and took us to the courthouse, where I was released without bail. I was angry that I missed my shift at work, and I needed a cigarette really bad. I was forty-five minutes away from home, and no one would come to get me. I walked to a four-way stop where I saw two guys standing. I asked one of them for a cigarette. I also asked where they were headed. They ended up giving me a ride and dropping me off close to home.

When you are going through a hard time, it's easy to believe you're the only one suffering. But the truth is, we all cover up our mistakes because we don't want others to see. No matter if you've been to jail, gotten mixed up with drugs or alcohol, or committed a crime, I promise you there is someone who has messed up even worse.

Here's another way of looking at it. If you are a baseball fan, you know that a .300 batting average is considered excellent. That means that the batter only gets a hit thirty percent of the time! The other seventy percent of the time, they strike out.

If professional baseball players only succeed thirty percent of the time, why should we expect any different from ourselves? Nobody gets it right all the time.

## LIE #4: SOMEDAY I'LL GET EVERYTHING RIGHT

We are constantly in a state of learning and growing. Even though I have been able to achieve many of my goals, I'm not finished yet.

One area where I'm still growing is balancing my time. I have a family, business, and other responsibilities that include taking care of my health. My family never complains, and they are very supportive. I'm thankful for that. But I don't always get it right.

Sometimes I feel like I'm failing as a wife. I'm not patient enough. Sometimes I take advantage of my husband because he's so supportive and does so much for me. I'm also trying to be more present when we have family time. So instead of being on my phone answering messages, I'll go for a walk with our dogs, my daughter, and my husband. The iPhone is put away and I'm going to be present in our conversation.

When we are working a lot, it's hard to be present because our minds are in so many places.

But it's not just the moments from day to day. It can be whole years of your life. Have you ever looked up from your work one day and thought, *Where did the last two years go?* That's what it can feel like when you're building a successful business.

It doesn't make it right. It doesn't mean it's okay to check out mentally from your family. But it does mean that it's something I'm working on.

The momentum in our business is very high right

now. Things are going well, and we are helping a lot of people. But it's a struggle to maintain my business at that level and still be present with my family.

Failure will be your constant companion on the road to success, and that is a good thing! There is no other way to achieve the dreams and the lifestyle you want.

## LIE #5: I HAVE TO DO THIS ALONE

We live in a culture that expects you to be strong. If you ask for help, some people might see you as weak and unworthy. But truthfully, all the meaningful things you accomplish in life will be done with other people's help.

Failure drives us deeper into ourselves. When things are not going well, we want to hide and pretend everything is okay. But this is the exact time we should ask for help.

Do you feel like you're going to be stuck with that extra weight forever? Do you feel like you'll be stuck in that job you hate? Do you feel like you'll never make more money, have that relationship you want, or achieve the big goal that's important to you?

Here is the key: you must have the right people around you. You must ask for help. You don't have to do this alone.

If you want to be a runner, you need to mingle with runners. You need people who will encourage you and give you tips. If you want to have a successful business, you need to mingle with business people who can give you good advice. If you want to be a better parent, you have to mingle with other parents who raise their kids in a way you want to emulate.

When I lost my dad, it was just my daughter and me. I put on fifteen to twenty extra pounds on my five-foot frame. That's two pants sizes! That is a lot of weight for someone my size. It was hard to find someone to support me. Even some of my own family would make fun of me and try to get me to go off my diet.

What goals are you trying to accomplish? You must surround yourself with people who are on the same path, who are picking themselves up every day, trying again and again. These are the people who will become your companions on the journey to success. You can find support groups for almost everything online or in person.

A great example of this is AA (Alcoholics Anonymous), an organization that has been around for decades. People who are struggling with alcohol addiction can go there and find a supportive community. For a more faith-based approach, you can look for a Celebrate Recovery program at a local church.

I have a friend named Candi who put on a lot of weight. She wanted to be healthier, but her husband was not supportive. He would tease her about her weight. It was almost impossible without being in a supportive environment.

I said, "Candi, you have to surround yourself with the right people. Do what you're passionate about. You need to connect with the right people who are involved in the same lifestyle you want to have." So, she started working out more and eventually met a friend who was doing CrossFit. Now, she is eating healthier and has a better lifestyle.

The next time I saw Candi, she had dropped twenty pounds! We went out for lunch, and she was super conscious of what she ate. She never used to do that.

It was all about the fact that she found something she loved to do and people who were interested in the same thing and supported her. Then it was so much easier for her to change.

Where do you want to be in one year? Two years? Five or ten years? Whatever your goals are, they won't happen by accident. You won't overcome your failures and setbacks on your own. Surround yourself with amazing people, and you'll have a much better chance of success.

As author Carol Dweck talks about in her book *Mindset*, there are two modes of thinking. One is a fixed mindset, and the other is a growth mindset. When you have a mindset of growth, you will constantly be stretching and developing.

That's the only way to learn from your failures. It's the only way to let them push you forward instead of holding you back.

As a little girl, I wanted to have special powers like Drew Barrymore in *Firestarter*. But it's just a movie, right? Everyone knows that special powers don't really exist.

Or do they?

The truth is, you do have special powers . . . if you

choose to use them. You have the power to learn from your mistakes and failures. Everyone has this power, but only a few people use it.

That power lets you use failure to get closer to your goals and begin creating a life you never thought possible. The only question is, are you going to use it?

## UNLOCK THE POSSIBILITIES

To learn from your failures and use them to help you grow:

1. What is the most significant area where you are failing right now? Write it down, and brainstorm ten things you can do to be more successful in that area.

2. We often feel like we are doing worse than everyone else. What are three areas of your life where you are doing better than most people?

3. What is the most significant area of your life you want to improve? Write down the name of one person who can help you. Call or email them within the next twenty-four hours and ask for help. (That action alone will give you immense power and motivation.)

## 5. FOCUS ON THE FUTURE

Every little girl wants to be a princess someday.

We dream of a knight in shining armor who will come to rescue us. He'll carry us away to live in a castle surrounded by everything we ever wanted. Life will be perfect, everyone will tell us how beautiful we are, and all our dreams will come true.

Most little girls know life is not a fairy tale. But they still hope for a stable family life and a good partner they can share life with.

My childhood was anything but a fairy tale. Most of the time, it was more like a horror movie.

I grew up with very little. I even spent one summer with no parents or supervision. My dad was in the hospital, and my mom was long gone. We had no food or supervision, and we would go to our neighbor's house for instant mashed potatoes. We didn't bathe the whole summer, and our scalps turned green. I was eight years old, living with my twin sister, eleven-year-old brother, and twelve-year-old sister.

We lived down a street that people called "the hood." I didn't dress nicely, and my clothes were never clean. My hair was always like a rat's nest, and I was so jealous of the girls with the pretty braids and ponytails. I wanted to be one of them so badly. Why couldn't I have a mom who would fix my hair, play dress-up, and do my makeup?

I was told we would never have nice things, and that's just the way the world was. People were lucky, and they had things because their parents gave it to them. You either had it, or you didn't.

My dad told us that if we worked hard enough, we might make it to the middle class. I never imagined that I could live in a nice house, drive a newer car, or make more than twelve dollars an hour. I was taught that there was a ceiling, and nothing above that ceiling was for me.

I was so broken, and so was my dad.

He would get angry at least four or five times every week—and not just a little. He hated life, and he hated us, or so it seemed. Dad was always yelling and cursing, calling us names. He often got violent with my older siblings when he lost his temper. My sister and I would cry (we were still very young). We got spanked with a belt, and it would hit our back and legs, but it never reached the violence my brother experienced, like being choked or slammed up against a wall. That came a few years later.

I remember the spit flying out of his mouth. It was so

gross and made me sick. He was *so* mean. I wouldn't want to come home because I was scared of what kind of mood he was in. If I got lucky, I was able to slide by while he was napping on the couch.

My dad lost his kidney function in his early thirties at the exact time my mom left. He was on dialysis and was always angry and tired. It was so difficult to focus at school. We were in survival mode.

My grades slipped in fourth grade, and I almost failed sixth grade. I had so many other things on my mind. My dad . . . my siblings . . . eating . . . feeling dirty . . . no one likes me . . . I'm not cool . . . I'm poor . . . everyone is better than me . . . my mom left because of us . . . is my dad mad today? . . . maybe he will be happy . . . maybe we can eat at Grandma's . . . TV dinners again with Salisbury steak and rock-hard mashed potatoes . . . maybe if we're really lucky, we'll get the one with the small hard brownie in it.

Those are the thoughts that occupied my mind. School was the least of my worries.

Other kids' parents didn't want them to hang out with us anymore. They called our mom a whore, and our dad was lost in his own world. We were those kids left with no one. We had no family, no friends, and the teachers thought we were unruly troublemakers. Maybe we were unruly, but it came from a place of survival and a lack of guidance.

We were beaten down and made to feel like we weren't good enough, like no one wanted us, and my dad was just *stuck* with us. We were more trouble than we were worth.

My dad was trying to get through the day, every single day. I hadn't heard from our mom in years, and if we did, it was normally a voice message saying, "Happy Birthday," on the wrong day. What mother forgets her kids' birthdays for years in a row, and then when she decides one year to call, it's the wrong day?

We were broken and needed help.

## YOU CAN CHANGE YOUR FUTURE

It's easy to focus on what you have lost. When you look back on your younger years, there are things you wish were different. Maybe there were things other people did to you. Maybe there were things others should have done but didn't. Or maybe there were things you did to yourself.

I can look back on my childhood and all the bad things that happened, and it feels like a giant loss. (And I've only touched the tip of the iceberg here!) I lost confidence in myself. I didn't think anybody would ever stay with me. I was terrified I would be abandoned or forgotten.

I never felt like I was good enough. I had no structure in my life. I don't even know what it meant to be engaged in high school.

There was so much I missed. So much I lost.

It is so easy to focus on the past. You can get lost for

hours, or even years, thinking about all the ways you have been hurt. But it doesn't change anything. Try as you might, you can't change the past. You can't resurrect what was lost.

Why do we spend so much emotional energy trying to fix the past? Why not invest that energy into changing the future?

I started to ask myself this question a few years ago. I realized that I needed to change my perspective. If I was going to live a bigger life, I had to stop looking backward. I needed to focus on the road ahead.

That's when life became fun!

I started to realize that I'm capable of something more. Even though I came from nothing, I figured out that hard work could take me anywhere I wanted to go. I went into network marketing and realized that working for myself, on my own hours, and on my own time, was the way to go. I started to make $4,000 a month with the first company where I worked. Many people think that is successful, but it's nothing compared to what we have been able to accomplish since then.

Before I got involved in network marketing, I always thought that you worked hard for minimum wage. Everyone I knew had a job where they punched a time clock. My dad told us to work hard and respect people. I was taught to respect your elders, be polite, and pay your bills.

That's all I was worried about. As long as I could pay my bills, I was content. Credit card debt was normal for me. Even though my dad always told me not to use credit cards, it was hard to resist. He encouraged us to save our money. But at that point in my life, I felt like saying, "What money? I don't even have any money left over from my check!"

But then I was presented with an opportunity with a network marketing company. I saw that it is a lot of hard work running your own business. Being an entrepreneur is not nine to five. Once I realized that I could do something myself without a boss and that I was earning a paycheck, I thought, *Wow...maybe I can do this!*

I doubted myself at first. Being an entrepreneur is not a normal thing. We're taught to go to college, get a job, and work for someone else. If you get a three percent raise, you are supposed to feel excited. That doesn't even cover the increase in insurance premiums. The corporate world dangles that carrot and makes you feel like a nine to five job is the best you can hope for.

Once I understood how marketing worked and realized I could do it, I started to see the possibilities. I saw people who were making five figures in a month. I wanted that to be me!

Have you ever gotten a bit of success and then felt terrified that it was all a fluke? It's like climbing a mountain. You get halfway up, you look down, and suddenly you lose your nerve.

That's what happened to me. I went backward for a moment because I was convinced it was not going to work out for me

I was focused on the past instead of looking toward the future. When you come from nothing, it's easy to convince yourself that's where you will end up. Remember the demons? They are always there, and they like to battle.

But you must remember; the future has not happened yet. It's not set in stone. *You can change your future.*

## IGNORANCE ON FIRE

No matter where you have come from . . . no matter what you have been through . . . no matter who told you that your dreams weren't possible . . . always remember that it *is* possible. Even when you doubt yourself and have moments of insecurity, keep moving forward and focusing on what's next.

There are opportunities all around you. All you have to do is open your eyes. I'm living proof that you can make a great living, be your own boss, and build a life that you love.

How did this happen? I put my head down and went to work. I call this "ignorance on fire." It's all about doing the job and worrying about the details later. In the first three months when I was building my business, it was not easy. There were people around me who said, "This is a waste of your time. It's a pyramid scheme. You're better off working for somebody else. That's guaranteed hours and money." There is risk, but it's about betting on yourself, and I will bet on me every time.

That would get me down for a while. I would feel sad and discouraged. But then I would wake up the next day, brush it off, and go for a run. Working out makes everything better. It gives you energy and helps you solve problems. It also helps relieve stress and clears your mind.

It's all about your mindset. It's knowing that if one person is doing something successfully, you can do it also.

Last fall, I worked like crazy for five months, and my business didn't move at all. But I stayed consistent and kept at it, doing the same things over and over again. This year has been our biggest ever.

When you do the right things consistently, you win in your business, health, and other areas of your life. Consistency wins every single time. That's how you stay focused on your future and the great things ahead.

As you're reading this chapter or thinking about this book's title—*Anything is Possible*—maybe you're feeling a bit cynical. Maybe you feel constrained by what's happened to you in the past. That is normal, and you're not alone.

It might not feel like it, but you have a better future ahead. Here's the thing: you have to *create* it. You have to create your future by focusing on the things that will make that future a reality.

You know all the grief, failure, or anger you feel inside? Those are not your enemies; those are your *allies*! Why? Because they can help you reach your goals. You can use your past to jumpstart your future.

Here are three things that have helped me stay

focused on the future. I didn't say they were easy . . . but they *work*!

## 1. TAKE THE STEPS TO ACHIEVE YOUR WHY

We talked about your *why* in a previous chapter. Once you have figured that out, what steps will get you there? It doesn't need to be complicated. Just use a simple checklist.

Maybe one of your steps is talking to ten people every day about your business. Maybe it's waking up earlier to go for a run. Maybe it's saving a certain amount of money. Whatever it is, make sure to write it down so you can see it every day.

When you first do that, it will feel exciting. Growth always does! But then you're going to hit some resistance when it gets hard. Be prepared for it, and stay consistent.

It's easy to make a checklist of things you need to do. But it's a lot harder to make a personal commitment to following through on those steps every single day. A commitment means that you will do it, no matter what. Whether or not you feel like it. Whether you're in the mood to do it. Whether or not you have the time.

Changing your life requires a personal sacrifice. Are you willing to commit?

## 2. FIND A ROLE MODEL

When you're changing your life and reaching for bigger goals, it helps to have an example of who you want to be. When I met my first husband, and then later met his mom, I immediately admired her. They were like a model family you see on TV.

I wanted to have a house like hers. I wanted to be the perfect wife and mother like she was. It's not that I wanted to be better than her. But she showed me that I could live a good life. She was like a mentor without even knowing it.

My mother-in-law was the complete opposite of my mother. My mom left my dad after his kidneys quit functioning. They started fighting when he began struggling with high blood pressure. I also suspect she had an affair. Our stable family never had a chance to exist, and I wanted to create that for my kids.

There my father was, struggling with his health, and my mom left him high and dry with four kids to raise. She also racked up debt on all his credit cards. In court, my father gave us kids to her, but she didn't want us. So, he ended up taking us. There were four of us kids—one set of twins, and neither parent wanted us. He didn't know how to handle things, and he loved my mom. He cared for her until the day he died.

You will have positive and negative role models in your life. It doesn't seem to make sense, but the negative role models can help you almost as much as the positive ones. The positive ones help you visualize what you should *become*, and the negative ones help you visualize what you should *avoid*.

My former mother-in-law was a huge influence on my life. I want you to find someone you admire so much that they become a reason for you to change.

## 3. KEEP GETTING UP

My dad taught me that if you get hurt, dust it off, get back up, and do it again. That's always been in the back of my head. My dad loved sports, so naturally, he used a lot of sports metaphors.

I try to tell myself that other people have it worse. There's no reason for me to stay down. If I want to live a different life, I can't stay where I am. I have to use that hurt and pain to improve my life and change my outcome.

The steps I've just listed have helped me become a better version of myself. I guarantee they will help you, too.

## YOU'RE NOT DEFINED BY YOUR PAST

There's one more thing we need to talk about before we close this chapter.

If you want to change your life and make your dreams a reality, you will come up against obstacles. Many of those obstacles will come from your self-limiting beliefs.

But some of the obstacles will come in the form of other people's bad advice.

Many people are still held captive by parents, teachers, siblings, or other people who told them they weren't worthy. Maybe they said you'll never amount to anything, you shouldn't go into that career, you're not college material, or you're not this or that.

When people try to hold you back (even if they have good intentions), look at how successful they are. Their level of success will tell you whether or not to take their advice. Just because they are not willing to take a risk doesn't mean you can't.

Do they seem happy? When people object to your success, that is usually their insecurities showing through. If they are not happy with their success, they will naturally want to tear you down. Misery loves company.

It's something I have dealt with as my business and success have grown. There are people from my hometown who won't talk to me anymore. I'm just at a different place in my life than they are. They're at the same bars doing the same things as they were in high school, rehashing their glory days.

Here's a little-known secret: your "glory days" were not so glorious. Your best days are ahead! That is, if you choose to make them that way.

We're not always going to do things that people agree with. We might have a different idea of success than they do. That's the way it is. Don't ever lose sleep over it. Just realize it's their inner demons and insecurities showing through.

People who are stuck in the past will always try to take away other people's futures. It has nothing to do with you.

Remember, you're *not* defined by your past, no matter what you might have done or what others have done to you. Every single thing that has happened to me has been fuel for my success. Every weakness can become a strength if you let it.

I used anger to become a stronger person and a better mother for my children. I used failure to help me get closer to the success I've been working towards.

There is no knight on a white horse, no Prince Charming who is coming to save you. But guess what? You don't need them. All you need is a daily commitment to reach your goals and keep going no matter what.

Nobody runs a race backwards. The only way to win a race is to keep moving forward.

You can build the life of your dreams if you're willing to put in the work. Every day you keep moving forward, you put another brick in the castle of your success.

With enough hard work and determination, fairy tales can come true after all.

## UNLOCK THE POSSIBILITIES

To help you focus on the future:

1. Decide on three to five next steps that will help you achieve your purpose. Don't over-complicate it. It doesn't need to be perfect. Keep it simple and write them down.

2. Who is a role model you want to be like? What do you admire in them? What would those qualities look like in your life?

3. What's your "rebound" factor? When you are knocked down, do you get back up again? Why or why not?

# 6. PRACTICE CONSISTENT HABITS

Have you ever had a moment when you realized your life was headed in the wrong direction, and you needed to make a radical change?

For me, that year was 2009.

I had just lost my dad the previous year and put on twenty pounds. That's not a life-altering amount of weight for many people. But for me, a person who is five feet tall, twenty pounds is a lot. I knew I had to make a change.

I started searching the internet and asking anyone I could find for ways to lose weight. I researched every aspect of weight loss I could think of. Everybody wants to see results right away, but I knew the results wouldn't come quickly. I knew that if I kept doing the work and putting in the effort, it would pay off.

For two solid months, I put in the work. No matter what distractions people threw in my way, I stayed consistent. I was doing everything right and going through all the motions, but the weight wasn't coming off.

Then one morning, I woke up, and it was almost like my pants fell off.

Of course, it didn't happen overnight, but it felt that way. It was the daily actions over those two months that produced the results. That's when I realized how much those small daily actions paid off.

That was eleven years ago. Once I realized the principle of consistency and began to live by it, great things started to happen in my life. I knew that even when bad things happened, everything would be okay if I just kept pushing forward.

The key ingredient to every achievement in my life is consistency—repeating the same actions over and over again until I conquer my goal. It is the single greatest thing you can do to achieve the life of your dreams.

I alluded to the weight loss story in the introduction to this book. Habits are such a critical element of success that I wanted to include it in this chapter as well. Consistent habits are not easy to develop, but they are doable.

In the rest of this chapter, you'll learn five steps to be more consistent in the actions that produce success.

## 1. CHANGE HOW YOU TALK TO YOURSELF

Maybe you have tried to make big changes in your life and failed. Let's take running, for example. If you have tried to develop a consistent running routine, but you keep failing, the answer is not just doing more of the same.

The answer is in how you talk to yourself.

Most people say, "I want to be a runner," which is great! But saying, "I want to be a runner" expresses a desire that you have—a goal. If you want to make better progress, say, "I *am* a runner." That completely changes how you think.

A person who *wants* to be a runner may or may not wake up at 6 a.m., put on their running shoes, and head out the door. But a person who *is* a runner will be more inclined to take action because running is a part of their identity.

How about you? What is a goal you have? What do you want to accomplish? What is a change in your life that has been just out of reach?

Let's take another example—losing weight. Maybe you've tried diets, eating healthier, or joining a program, but you can't seem to stick with it and get the pounds off.

How do people in this situation normally talk to themselves? They'll say things like:

- "I'd really love to get this weight off."
- "It's so hard to eat healthier."
- "Why bother trying? I'll just fail anyway."

Any of those sound familiar?

This isn't just a problem of habits or effort. It's an

identity problem. Instead of framing the issue as something you will accomplish "someday," it's more effective to think like this:

- "I'm a person who eats healthy."
- "I make great choices with my food."
- "I have energy and feel great because I take care of my body."

See how talking to yourself the right way can make a big difference? The change you desire becomes something you can live out *right now* instead of wishing upon a star.

While we're on the topic of food, let me say one more thing since many people struggle in this area. In Western culture, we have a messed-up relationship with food. We treat food only as a source of pleasure. But remember, food is fuel for your body, nothing more.

You can make healthy food taste good, and of course, that is pleasurable. But when you eat, you fuel your body to help keep it moving and operative in a peak state.

Doughnuts aren't going to help you with that! They may taste great, but they are going to work against you. If you struggle with junk food or eating healthy, you need to work on your relationship with food.

If you cut out sugar for a couple of days, you'll quickly see how much energy you have throughout the day. You'll feel so much better and won't even want sugary foods.

But as soon as you have those foods again, you'll go right back to your old habits. It's so addicting.

If you're struggling with exercise or eating healthier, or any other goal for that matter, the first place to start is by changing how to talk to yourself.

## 2. EMBRACE HARD WORK

Here is the cold, hard truth. No one is coming to save you. No one is going to pay your bills. No one is building a dream home for you, cooking your dinner, or going to work for you.

Dreams only work when *you* work. Dreams only work when *you* make a decision. You must decide that *you* are responsible for your outcome. No excuses. Put your head down and *go to work*!

You will fail. You will get stuck. You will feel tired. Many times, you will feel lost and alone. You have to work when no one is clapping for you. That is when you will live your dreams! Dreams are just goals that you haven't reached yet.

I never, in a million years, thought I would be living the life I'm living. It was a pipe dream—a dream I didn't think would ever become a reality. It's a life I used to envy. Then one day, I told myself, "Enough! I am doing this!"

I didn't say, "I will try." I said, "I am doing this!" There's a big difference between "try" and "do." Remember Yoda from *The Empire Strikes Back* and his famous words to Luke Skywalker when he was training to be a Jedi?

"Do or do not. There is no try."

There is no try. You either do it, or you don't—end of discussion.

My life seemed to start off badly and kept getting worse. My Mom left, school was a train wreck, so I quit, I got married, that turned into a divorce and $50,000 worth of debt, and my dad died. Any of those experiences could have broken me.

But nothing magic happened. There was no white knight who came to save me. I just changed my mindset.

Success is not luck or magic. Success is earned. It takes consistency, hard work, and the will to keep going when no one cheers you on. It takes changing the way you think and having goals with action behind them. It means not quitting when things get tough. And trust me, there will be plenty of those times.

Many people believe that success is about being smart. But just because you didn't go to college (or even finish high school) doesn't mean you're not smart. It could mean that some serious things were going on, and school wasn't a priority.

Success isn't based on formal education. It's based on drive, grit, determination, and above all, hard work. When you embrace the hard work, you will naturally be more consistent, which leads to more success.

## 3. TRAIN FOR THE BIG DAY

The problem with trying to build consistency into your life is that it's . . . well, it's a lot of *hard work*, as I just mentioned. So, what can you do to ensure that you're putting in the hard work regularly?

The best way I know how is to commit to something that requires you to train.

I ran my first marathon in Champagne, Illinois, in 2015. I trained for seventeen weeks. I would run three miles on Monday, five miles on Wednesday, two miles on Friday, and do my long run on Saturday. I repeated this routine every single week until I had run twenty miles on a Saturday. Now I was ready to run 26.2 miles, and it felt amazing. I was also thankful my older sister was running with me.

On the day of the run, we were so excited, and nothing was going to stop us. Nothing, that is . . . until we got to mile sixteen, and it started pouring down rain. It was raining so hard that they *canceled the race*. The weather was so bad they had to bus us off the road.

All my hard work and training seemed to be for nothing. I could have allowed that experience to defeat me, but on the car ride home, we decided to run the next race, which was two weeks away.

I went back home and started where I left off. The first race was a flat course, and that's why we chose it. The second one was at Starved Rock State Park (in northern Illinois), which is not flat at all!

Partway through the race, it began to storm. We thought, *Oh no, not again!* We heard through the grapevine that the organizers were talking about canceling the race. We even stopped and talked to a police officer on the race route, and he indicated they might cancel it and send all the volunteers home.

I looked at my sister and said, "We ain't stopping, even if all the volunteers leave. We are running to the finish line with or without a medal!" Some people did take busses to the finish line. But my sister and I ran the whole thing, even through the storm and the lightning.

At one point, we ran across a metal bridge. I remember saying, "We're going to get struck by lightning!" We ran across that bridge so freaking fast. My husband, Brent, and my brother-in-law were waiting for us across the bridge with mini Payday candy bars because they wanted to help us finish.

My sister was doing a walk/run method. Around mile twenty-three, I told her that I couldn't walk and had to run. She had a partner, and I knew she wasn't going to be by herself. So, I took off running, and they got stuck behind a train. I finished the race by myself at five hours, twenty minutes. My sister came in behind me a while later.

Finishing that race made me realize that you can do anything if you train for it hard enough. If you're willing to put in the work, it becomes easy.

Running a marathon isn't as difficult as many people think. Most people think running a marathon is nearly impossible. After all, it's 26.2 miles! However, it wasn't that big of a deal for me mentally because I was already running twenty miles at a time. I trained well and was prepared.

I did all this as a smoker. I had been a smoker for more years than I hadn't. I smoked from 1994 up until three and a half years ago. I ran the marathon as a smoker. You couldn't tell me something was impossible!

However, I quit smoking when I competed in my first bodybuilding competition. I didn't want one thing to prevent me from winning. Smoking was the only thing that "had me." It was the only thing that could control me.

When I was able to quit smoking, I knew that I could seriously do anything.

Maybe running or bodybuilding isn't your thing. But like me, maybe something "has you." Is there a bad habit or a hang-up that's holding you back? If so, commit to a "big day" such as a race or other event. Then start training and preparing. That is one of the best ways to be more consistent in your life. The training kicks in and makes personal change much easier.

## 4. GROW YOUR GRIT

Grit is not a word we use very often, but it's essential if you want to be more consistent and successful.

Here's how I define grit: no matter what happens in

your life, no matter how hard it gets, you keep going. You don't quit when other people throw in the towel.

If you've ever used sandpaper, you know what grit feels like. Sandpaper is rough to the touch, but when it comes in contact with wood, it makes the wood smooth. A carpenter would never do woodworking without using sandpaper to finish the job. The item made of wood wouldn't be complete and ready for presentation.

That's what grit does in your life—it makes you "ready for presentation." It gets you ready for what life throws at you.

Grit was ingrained in me from a young age. I've always been in survival mode. The only thing that helped me keep going when life kept bringing me down is pure grit. That stubborn quality of never giving up helped me get over the humps to the next level. It helped me get out of my comfort zone and up to higher levels of success.

But what if you don't have grit? What if you're timid, passive, or don't feel motivated? There are two ways to develop more grit.

The first is by experiencing adversity. There are times in life when something happens, and you simply decide you don't want to live that way anymore. Life slaps you around, and you realize you must fight back to survive.

You find out who you really are when you face adversity. You either stay down for the count, or you get back up as many times as it takes.

That's why it's hard for rich kids to develop grit. Most of the time, they have everything in life handed to them, and they can't develop grit. They haven't worked their "persistence" muscle.

There's a second way to develop more grit—by challenging yourself. It's pushing yourself harder, overcoming obstacles, and creating challenges for yourself. If you're not willing to push yourself more, you won't develop more grit—end of story.

Some people wither at the slightest hint of pain. They'll never have the grit and determination to achieve more success.

I also believe this is why you shouldn't spoil your kids. You should let them have a little adversity in life. It's okay for them to get yelled at, have some difficult chores, and work through tasks that seem impossible. Let them fight through it because that's the only way they will develop a tougher shell.

Some people don't develop this until later in life. They will have a great life until twenty-six, twenty-seven, or twenty-eight, and then something will happen. Maybe their husband or wife cheats on them. Maybe a parent dies. Something out of the blue happens, and bam! They're slapped down onto the cold pavement.

In those moments, you have to wake up and ask yourself, "Do I keep moving on?" or "Do I let myself fold into nothingness?"

Nobody wishes for those moments, but we should be thankful for them. Those are the times when we develop perseverance and grit to help us move on.

## 5. DON'T QUIT

I don't want you to get the impression that I have it all together. I don't. There are still areas where I'm learning to be more consistent.

For example, I'm not always consistent with my daughter, Savannah. I'm not always present in her life when I need to be. If she needs something, wants to talk about something, or share something, I'm not always mentally present. I'm often checked out.

It's like I'm listening, but I'm thinking of something else. And normally, it has to do with my business. I'm working on that, but I would say that it's made me miss out on many things in her life. There are things I'll pick up on and then say, "Oh my goodness, I didn't realize you felt that way."

Sometimes it feels as if she's growing up without me even noticing because I'm not present. We have a good relationship, but I could do so much better. I could be more consistent.

Here's what I'm doing to improve in this area: I'm creating a better work schedule and spending more time in meditation and personal development. When I do those things, they improve every area of my life, including being a mom.

I'm forcing myself to do a little bit more because there are times when I'm working out when I used to do a lot of self-development. But as I'm writing this in the summer of 2020, the gyms are closed, and I've had to watch the workout on my phone instead of plugging into self-development. I'm not getting as much of it as I used to.

To compensate for that, I'm forcing myself to do it in the car or during other parts of the day to get more of it in. The goal is to be more present when I'm spending time with her instead of being preoccupied with business.

I'm a work in progress, that's for sure. I can do better, and I'm working on it. I realize that to be financially successful; I have to sacrifice. But I also need to remember that my daughter will be out of the house before I know it. I'll regret that time with her that I missed.

Maybe you're dealing with a similar situation as a parent. Maybe it's a totally different problem you're working through. Whatever it is, don't quit. Don't stop growing and becoming a better version of yourself.

You're worth it, and your family is worth it.

## KEEP PUTTING IN THE REPS

So, there you have it: five ways you can be more consistent in your life. If you follow these principles, you *will* see results. It won't happen overnight because change takes time.

But once you build momentum and keep putting in the reps, it will feel like success happens overnight. You reach a tipping point when all your hard work starts to pay off.

It's not something you do once. You have to do it every day. Even now, in my business, I'm doing things every day to produce results that will show up in a couple of months. If I wake up one day a couple of months from now, and I don't have the results I want, it's because I didn't put in the consistent effort two months ago.

Have you ever heard the phrase, "I don't want easy, I just want possible"? That's the kind of attitude we have to embrace if we're going to have the life we want.

It's possible . . . but not easy. The harder you work, and the more consistent action you take, the sweeter the rewards.

## UNLOCK THE POSSIBILITIES

To be more consistent:

1. Think about your biggest goal for this year. How do you talk to yourself about your goal? Use "I am" statements instead of "I wish" or "I want."

2. Make a public commitment to a big goal, such as running a race. You will naturally prepare and train for it, and in the process, you will become more consistent.

3. Answer this question honestly: Do you have grit? If you don't, why not? What is a challenge you can give yourself to help you develop more perseverance and grit?

## 7. CHOOSE YOUR FRIENDS WISELY

One of the greatest movies of all time is 1939's *The Wizard of Oz*. Almost everyone has seen it, so there is no need to re-hash the plot. I have always been fascinated by the items each of Dorothy's traveling companions needed from the Wizard. Why? Because each one represents something you need on your journey to the dream life.

The Scarecrow needed a brain. And who doesn't? A brain is pretty important. It represents the skills and knowledge you need to survive and thrive in the world.

The Tin Man needed a heart. He wanted to be able to give and receive love. Without love, your life and work have no soul. You forget why you are doing what you're doing, and whom you're doing it for.

The Cowardly Lion needed courage. Out of these three elements—brain, heart, and courage—the last one is the most misunderstood. It's also the least valued. You can have all the brains and love in the world, but if you don't have the courage to push through obstacles and make hard choices, you'll be stuck forever.

There is no area where this is truer than your relationships. As you're building the life of your dreams, you'll need courage to make tough choices about the people who surround you. This area of success doesn't get enough attention. You hear a lot about personal development and skills, which are important. You also hear a lot about having passion for what you do or a career you love, and that's also important.

However, you don't hear as much about choosing the right people to go with you on your journey.

Dorothy wouldn't have made it to Emerald City or defeated the Wicked Witch of the West without her friends. And just like Dorothy, you won't be able to reach your potential without the right people around you. It's a hard truth that many people can't accept because they don't like conflict. They don't like disappointing other people or making them unhappy.

Your network is a crucial area of success. In this chapter, you'll learn how to reject low standards, raise your standards, and network with successful people. You must choose your friends wisely.

It's not hard to understand, but it does take courage. Before we talk about the importance of rejecting low standards, let me share a perspective on this lesson I wish I would have known in my younger days.

## MY TROUBLED TEEN YEARS

As a teenager, all I wanted to do was escape my family. I started seriously rebelling in the seventh grade. I began smoking and fighting with my dad a lot, even to the point where I asked to live with my mom.

She lived in a two-bedroom apartment with my older sister and her boyfriend. We had to sleep either in her bed or on a day bed. My mom was never home, and there was no food. We would steal laundry money just to buy a cheeseburger at McDonald's. If someone called, we had to refer to her as "Aunt Becky" because she had multiple boyfriends who didn't know she had kids. We only lived there for a couple of months.

In the eighth grade, we moved back in with my dad. I made the cheerleading squad and wanted to improve my life but didn't have the support. Smoking had become a full habit, and I began skipping school. That's when I started using illegal drugs, including pot, which my brother introduced me to.

My twin sister got pregnant, and we barely spoke to my dad. We had no adult supervision, and we took full advantage of the situation. We knew we didn't have to go to school or do anything else we didn't want, for that matter.

I was bagging oranges for money to buy pot and started hanging out with a new crowd who used more drugs and alcohol. One of my new "friends" was a thirty-year-old drug dealer. I tried acid for the first time and thought I was going to die. We took three hits, and the horrible feeling wouldn't go away. We were out in the middle of nowhere, and the car battery died, so we had to call a friend's parents to come and get us. My dad had no idea where I was and didn't care.

I had to repeat the eighth grade due to all my missed school. They were going to hold me back again for a third year, but I went to summer school to avoid that. My sister and I were then both freshmen in high school, and she had a one-year-old baby. The pressure was too much, and she dropped out.

I wanted to do well in school that time, but I didn't know how to study or be a student. I was so focused on my home life, eating, and trying to survive that school didn't take priority. Real life took over, so I also dropped out of school.

I couldn't get a driver's license in Illinois because I hadn't completed driver's education. I used my mom's address, which was in Missouri, and I was able to get my license. My dad said that if I didn't go to school, I had to work. I became a major pothead, smoking all day every day. I carried it with me at all times. Pot was the only way I could cope with life.

One time, I went to hang out with my brother and his friend, and they introduced me to crystal meth. I did it for the first time and was up all night. I also started hanging out with a guy who was a drug dealer. His brother had dealt drugs and died of a heroin overdose.

After my period of using meth, I hooked up with an older crowd and started using coke.

I did these drugs for a solid three or four months. Once I was up for three full days. It got so bad I had to start smoking drugs since my nose was so messed up that I couldn't snort it anymore. I weighed eighty pounds, didn't live at home, and I don't remember eating. There was so much partying that it was all a fog. I can't remember how I got to places, or how I got home. I'm surprised I wasn't murdered or raped.

After that day when my body froze up and I thought I was dying, I decided I would never touch drugs again. I packed up my stuff and moved back home. I ended up getting a full-time job at a grocery store. I never talked to the drug dealer again.

I came out alive on the other side of this horrible period in my teen years, but just barely. There were so many times I could have gotten into far more serious trouble or even died. I wish someone had told me about the incredible power of relationships to drag you down or lift you up.

## THE COURAGE TO REJECT LOW STANDARDS

Your relationships have a massive impact on your success. Why is that? Because your friends help determine how you think. They affect your mindset. Jim Rohn famously said that we are the average of the five people you spend the most time with, which is true. You can't grow beyond the level of the people around you. That's why it's vital to reject the low standards of other people in your life.

I have a friend who grew up in the same neighborhood as me. We hung around with many of the same people and basically have the same background. We were raised around the types of people whose standards and expectations never grew outside of where they were. They believed everything they heard and accepted life as it was given to them.

However, there are certain things in her life that she views as acceptable, but I do not. For example, I was recently with this friend and her son. He started verbally attacking me, and the whole situation was terrible and very dysfunctional.

I told my friend, "I left all this dysfunction behind me. I don't have to live this way anymore. If you want to accept this behavior, that's fine, but I cannot be around it. I cannot have this dysfunction in my headspace."

This type of situation affects me negatively. If I accept this behavior, I'm lowering my standards and giving the impression that it's okay. My friend believes there was nothing wrong with what happened, and she never even apologized for her son's behavior. She said, "I'm sorry I can't cater to you like everyone else."

That is where people get stuck. They feel that having common decency means "catering" to someone. That's not catering—it's simply being a kind human being.

It blows my mind how some people get stuck in their low standards. They don't respect themselves.

You, on the other hand, must respect yourself. If you lower your standards and allow people to treat you in a certain way, you will eventually become just like them. It's like a person who moves to a different region and, before long, starts talking with a new accent.

What types of behavior should you reject? There are several "red flags" in a relationship. These behaviors show you a person who is going to drag you down instead of taking you higher.

*Red Flag #1: How they talk about others.*

Let's say you have a friend named Linda who is talking smack about Bethany. Linda keeps running Bethany down and saying all kinds of nasty things about her. You aren't sure what to believe.

But then a short time later, you go out with a group that includes Linda and Bethany, and they appear to be great friends. Then you understand that Linda is a gossip, and you wonder what kinds of nasty things she is saying about *you* behind your back.

A person who gossips about others is like poison. They contaminate everything they touch.

*Red Flag #2: How they respond to kindness.*

That is like the flip side of gossip. A person who gossips and drags other people down cannot stand it when other people are kind, generous, or thoughtful.

For example, my husband, Brent, prepares my coffee in the morning when he makes his. Sometimes, I ask him to wake me up (even though I have my own alarm clock). He'll also make my protein shakes and do other little favors for me. Brent is always willing to help because he knows I keep very busy running my business.

That type of behavior will annoy people who are not thoughtful or caring. They cannot stand it when others show kindness. Whenever you're out with a group of people, you can always tell the unkind ones because they react negatively to another person's kindness. They usually couch their negative attitude in the form of sarcasm or making fun of others who are kind.

*Red Flag #3: How they treat their spouse in public.*

Have you ever been out with another couple, and one of them keeps criticizing the other one? It makes everyone uncomfortable. You begin to wonder what kind of things happen in private if they are willing to be so critical in public.

There can be many other red flags, and I encourage you to think about some you have seen in others. What is the behavior you will not tolerate?

Decide in your heart what you will and will not tolerate. Then, figure out how to withdraw from those relationships as best you can. I've had to do this over the years. I had a friend who was increasingly negative, especially where it concerned religious and political matters. I try not to judge people, and everybody has a right to their own opinion, but the constant negativity was dragging me down.

I withdrew from that person, and we didn't talk for a couple of years. It wasn't a sudden ending. I just gradually spoke to them less and less. But I would occasionally check in with them to see how they were doing.

There's no need to make an enemy where you don't need to. So many people see the world in strict black and white terms. In their world, people are either "in" or "out." But you can create space in relationships and reduce negative people's influence on you without totally breaking things off.

You would think that with most people, you'd be able to sit down and have an adult conversation about a variety of topics. But there are so many who are close-minded. They are going to think whatever they think, and there's no changing it. So, it's better to move on.

If you are in a growth mode, and those around you are stuck in their ways or are negative, it's not going to help you.

As I mentioned in the last chapter, this is the part of success many people cannot tolerate. They don't want conflict, and they want everyone to like them. You don't have to make enemies, but you do have to make choices about your relationships.

You're not going to make everyone happy. That's a fact. But if you want to achieve more, you need to take off the shackles of low standards that may be holding you back.

## THE COURAGE TO RAISE YOUR STANDARDS

The hardest part of this process is rejecting low standards. Once you have the courage to do that, it's much easier to be more successful because you have started to get the obstacles out of the way. Then, you can begin making real progress!

But it's not enough just to reject low standards. You must intentionally build relationships with people who have higher standards. These are people who demand more of themselves, and in turn, lift up everyone around them.

There's an old saying that goes, "A rising tide lifts all ships." If you have spent your whole life around "low tide" people, it's refreshing to start spending more time around people who bring in the high tide.

What qualities should you look for in these kinds of people with higher standards?

One of the most important qualities is that they motivate and inspire you. People do this in different ways. Some give speeches; some write books; some run companies; some are well-known, and some are not.

But the one thing they have in common is that they inspire you by living at a higher level. Not only with their actions, but with their words as well. "High tide" people are encouragers. They speak positively and always find ways to lift others.

Another essential quality is that they cheer you on. They clap when you do well. That is a sign of a person who has inner security. They don't feel threatened by other successful people.

An insecure person feels intimidated by other successful people because they believe there is only so much success to go around. But truly successful people know that success breeds success. When they cheer you on, it comes from a place of security and abundance.

You can tell what kind of person it is by what they talk about. People with low standards gossip about others. They focus on other people's problems and how bad they are. They are only interested in cutting other people down because it makes them feel better about themselves.

People with higher standards focus on helping others. They'll talk about how we can go out and make another $20,000 this month instead of talking about Sally because her husband had an affair.

The issue of high standards is most apparent when it relates to your spouse. You can still be successful without a supportive spouse, but it's harder and not as much fun. I am living proof of this because I have a supportive husband, Brent, and life is so much more fun with him!

Brent takes off the stress. He's able to pick up the slack. If I'm having a busy month and falling behind, he is there to help. He works full-time, so it's a lot to ask him to cook dinner every night or do laundry. He makes my life easier when it comes to business. If there is a way he can help, he's always willing to pitch in. We're getting ready to send out 270 gifts to my customers. We do that twice a year, and he's going to help me with that because it gives me anxiety.

But it's not only in the business. Brent also supports me in other areas of life. If I'm struggling with keeping up with my fitness lifestyle, he jumps in and helps me.

If I say, "Man, I'm just not liking the way I look right now," he'll say, "Okay, you know what? Let's do it together." It's easier if he does it with me. I can still do it without him, but it's easier to stay committed to working out and eating healthy if my husband is doing it too.

Many guys would not be willing to eat vegetables and meat for two weeks because their poor wife wants to lean out a little bit. He's a good sport.

## WHAT IF MY SPOUSE ISN'T SUPPORTIVE?

You might be reading this and thinking, "Sadie, that's great. But my husband is not supportive at all." And I hear you. I really do. It's a tough situation.

I know this can happen to both men and women, but I'll focus on the women's perspective. I have a friend who has made about $50,000 each of the last few months. It's crazy how much money she has made! But her husband is very needy.

When you are working towards something, and your

husband is not supportive, you need to have a real conversation with him. Let him know. Talk to him about what's at stake and how your business will change your family's life.

It's hard for me to understand how a person can love somebody so much and not support their dreams. And the older I get, I'm a little more selfish and think that we have one life to live, so I should enjoy mine. I wouldn't expect Brent to settle for less than what he deserves. Why should he sacrifice his happiness? Everybody deserves to have their happiness, whether you're married or not.

The best course of action is to express how much you are enjoying your life and business. Then hope and pray that they get on the bandwagon when they see how happy you are. It's also important not to compare your husband to other husbands. That's a great way to make him feel inadequate and push him away further, which is not what you want.

## THE COURAGE TO CONNECT WITH SUCCESSFUL PEOPLE

So far, we have talked about courage in rejecting low standards, courage in raising your standards by choosing the right kind of friends, and the importance of having a supportive spouse. It takes courage to change and reach for a better life.

In this final section, I want you to see the importance of connecting with highly successful people. That also requires courage because most people are afraid to reach out to people who live and operate at a higher level. It can feel scary and intimidating.

I have made a habit of reaching out to very successful people to pick their brains and ask questions. If someone is doing something right in their life or business, you can learn from them. You are never too good to learn, and you should be growing and developing every day.

We are often intimidated by successful people because we believe they are better or smarter than us. But that may not be the case; it might just be a matter of them "getting there" first. They have probably been involved in their business for longer. It's important for you to acknowledge where you are and understand that everyone has to start somewhere.

Reach out to people who can help you, who have wisdom to share. Ask them how they did it and what they are doing. How did they get there? What are they doing for personal development? Get in meetings with those people, hear how they talk with their teams and employees, and see what they are doing. You will learn a ton.

I recently met with somebody who has made $4 million in the last three years. She's a good friend of mine and the one who brought me into this business. She's super smart yet also very kind. She has been my mentor.

A lot of people worry that successful people are unapproachable because of their success. But that's not always the case. I have sometimes been afraid to approach these people because I felt intimidated. But remember, they are human just like we are. At one time, they were at the same place we are, or maybe even worse.

One such person was Amy (not her real name). Amy has a very successful business, and I wanted to reach out to her to ask some business-related questions. She was very nice, but I was intimidated. We had a phone conversation, and she was helpful.

Amy turned me down three times when it came to a business offer, but we remained friends. We checked in on each other for a while, and she did end up joining me in that business, and she's super successful. Amy is very nice, very down-to-earth, and not judgmental at all.

But here's one thing that was surprising; I thought she was way more successful than she was. Often, we think that people are way more successful than they are just because of what you see on social media or how they talk about themselves. Then you get to know them, and you realize they weren't as successful as you assumed. It's easy to get a picture in your head of someone's level of success based on their social media feed.

I'm not saying this to downplay Amy's success. Instead, I'm driving home the point that you shouldn't feel intimidated by someone's appearance of success. First of all, they may not be at the level you think. And second, even if they are, there is a good chance they are very nice and helpful.

You don't need to connect with every single person. Once you get into an industry, you'll discover some people you don't want to follow. Maybe they don't have your values, or you don't jive with the way they do business. That's totally cool. Nothing wrong with that.

But there will be others you want to connect with. Follow them on social media, read what they write, listen to their podcast (if they have one), or interviews they have done on other podcasts. Then don't be afraid to reach out to them.

One of the best ways to connect with successful people is by sending direct messages on social media. But when you do this, don't start by asking for something. It's helpful to say something like, "Just wanted you to know I read [insert something they've written or created] and loved it. Thanks for your insights. I appreciate what you're doing." That type of interaction creates value for them and begins a conversation.

Far too many people start by asking for something from successful people. That gets the relationship started on the wrong foot. It's much better to lead by adding value first and being kind. Kindness and generosity win every time!

We've covered a lot of ground in this chapter. But I felt it was important to go in-depth into this area of relationships because many get tripped up here. Your relationships will literally make or break you. You have skills, passion, and opportunities, but if you don't have the right people in your life, you'll be sunk.

You can do this! All it requires is a little courage.

## UNLOCK THE POSSIBILITIES

To take your relationships to the next level:

1. Make a list of the low standards you are not willing to put up with. It may seem like a simple exercise, but when you put it on paper, it has a powerful effect of making these "intolerables" more concrete in your mind.

2. Now, make a list of the qualities you most want in your friends and social circle. Do your current friends possess these qualities? If not, what should you do about it? And most importantly, do *you* have these qualities?

3. Who are three successful people in your industry or field that you'd like to connect with? Make a plan to connect with each of them in the next seven days by sending a direct message on social media.

# 8. TAKE CARE OF YOUR BODY

I met my husband, Brent, while doing what I love the most—hitting the gym. I always tell people that if you focus on what makes you happy, you will meet the most amazing people along the way because they enjoy the same things.

Well, it's true. I met my best friend while doing something I love. I wasn't even looking for a relationship. I had been single for three years and was happy to remain that way.

Brent pushed his way in and made a perfect addition to our lives. We were married in March of 2014. We had a small but beautiful wedding. A couple of years later, in 2016, I decided to train for my first full marathon. It was an amazing accomplishment that gave me a whole new level of confidence. I ran the marathon with my older sister, who was my favorite running partner at that time.

By 2017, I was a bit burned out on running and took another path. I decided to compete in my first bikini competition. I mean, why not? Brent competed with me. It was nice to have someone cut weight with me. It is easier when you have a partner who is eating the same way as you. That is totally normal behavior for Brent. He believes in me, and he always has my back. It's important to have a partner that makes you a better person.

That was Brent's second show and my first. It consumed me. While you're preparing, it's all you can think about. And rightfully so, because it's a huge commitment. I did seventeen weeks of cutting and two workouts per day. It was serious business.

I placed second and sixth. I was thrilled with those results since it was my first show. But to top it all off, I quit smoking during this same time. I had smoked since 1994 when I was fourteen years old. I had smoked more of my life than I hadn't!

I never thought I would kick the habit. I enjoyed smoking. But the best thing I ever did was quit. There is nothing like the amazing feeling of being *free*. Nothing owns you, and you have complete control over your life and your habits.

Which brings me to the topic of this chapter—getting healthy. I want you to be *free*. I want you to experience the joy that comes when you realize that *anything is possible*. I want you to have the energy to achieve *every dream* in your heart.

But it's much harder to do when you don't feel well or don't have the stamina to make it through the day. That's why I've included this chapter—because your health is an essential part of achieving success.

In the previous chapter, you learned why it's easier to transform your life when you have a great community surrounding you. As you read this chapter and consider the changes you want to make in your health, I encourage you to enlist the help of a friend or your spouse.

## THIS CHAPTER IS FOR YOU (YES, YOU!)

When it comes to health and nutrition, you're probably thinking you're the exception, right? Maybe you agree with everything else in this book, but this chapter is the one you're struggling with. Why? Because many people struggle with their health. It's an easy area to neglect.

You can succeed in every other area of your life, but if you're not healthy, you're "poor." No matter what size or age you are, health is vital for your quality of life.

Many believe that only young people work out or that it's normal to be overweight and out of shape. But it's not. If you're not healthy, you won't have the quality of life that you would if you were active at least thirty minutes a day, six days a week.

I recently took my daughter, Savannah, to the doctor who helped us work through some issues related to nutrition and acne. The doctor emphasized the importance of being active, no matter what your age. Many people in their 70s, 80s, and beyond don't have as much energy as they want because they ignored their health in earlier years.

When I talk about fitness or health, I'm talking about how you feel about yourself. There are objective standards and measurements for health, but it's more about your self-image. How do you feel about yourself? Do you feel lean and energetic or mushy and lethargic?

You get one shot at this life, one go-round on this planet Earth. So why not make it the best journey possible?

It's not just about eating healthy food or working out every day. Those are important factors, but the bigger picture is all about being a whole, healthy person.

I'm not here to preach at you. I'm here to help you pay attention to your fitness and take care of the only body God has given you. If you feel healthy, you usually feel better about yourself. That translates to your family life, business, relationships, finances, and every other area.

Before we talk about specific ways to get started, let's take a look at why health is important in the first place.

## THE BENEFITS OF GETTING HEALTHY

If you Google, "Why should I get healthy?" you'll come up with over *one billion* search results. I'm not going to give you that many reasons here. But I do want to highlight three reasons why I choose to live a healthy lifestyle. I'm sure you will resonate with these also.

*1. My daughter is proud of me.*

Every parent should be proud of their kids, but have you ever thought of it the other way around? What about your kids being proud of *you*?

Your kids may not say this out loud, but how you present yourself to their friends does make a difference. Savannah has mentioned that she is proud to show me off to her friends because I stay in shape.

If you're out of shape or don't take care of yourself, your kids might feel embarrassed to introduce you to their friends. That's hard to hear but true.

*2. I have a better quality of life.*

It's not just about living longer. It's also about living a higher-quality life where you can do more things and enjoy it more. When you have more energy, you have more options.

Think about a recent time when you felt sluggish and out of shape. How did that affect your relationships? Your motivation to work hard? Your creativity? Your enjoyment of life? A lack of energy affects every area of your life.

It's essential to have energy as a parent, but even more as a grandparent! I'm not a grandma yet, but one day I hope to be. And I want to have all the energy I need to play with my grandkids.

One of the most significant benefits of running is that it feels like therapy. Running is the cheapest counselor you will ever have. When you run, your mind can find solutions to problems, come up with new ideas, and have an outlet for your stress.

Health and fitness improve every area of your life. That's why exercise is one of the best time investments you can make.

*3. I have more self-confidence.*

When you are healthier, your clothes fit better, and you look better. You naturally have more self-confidence. But it's more than just your appearance.

Getting healthier is one of the hardest things you will ever do. When you can crush those goals, it sets you up for success in every other area of your life.

One of my friends, Karen, has lost 187 pounds. She was one of those extremely heavy girls who most people assume will never get the weight off. She's had setbacks, but she pushed through them. Karen is now a health coach and regularly trains at the gym. She still has some weight to lose, but she's lost the equivalent of a full-grown man!

That's a massive accomplishment (no pun intended). When you conquer a goal that big, you have the confidence to charge through anything. You think, *No problem.*

*I've lost 187 pounds—nothing is impossible!* Karen threw out her excuses and simply got to work.

I haven't lost 187 pounds like Karen, but health and fitness have given me the confidence to accomplish goals I never thought possible. I can do the same for you.

## THINGS YOU'LL NEED TO GIVE UP

It's time to get real for a second. It isn't going to be easy. You already knew that, right? But let's get brutally honest about some things you'll need to give up if you want to get healthier.

Here's the thing: you can't add something positive to your life without letting something else go. When you embark on a journey of health, you're going to come up against old habits and mindsets. When you know that up front, it's easier to let go of the old to make room for the new.

Here are a few things that need to go:

*1. Late nights.*

One of the things I sacrifice is late nights. I typically don't stay up late to binge-watch Netflix. If I want to get up and work out in the morning, I need to go to bed by 10:00 p.m. Even then, it can still be a struggle to get up by 7:00 a.m.

That happened just this morning! I was supposed to

get up at 6:00 a.m. and run with Brent, but I slept until 7:00 and ran by myself. I still got my run in.

Can you still stay up late and go running anytime you want? Of course. But it's harder. When you exercise first thing in the morning, it sets you up for success for the rest of the day. The longer the day goes on, the less likely you are to exercise.

*2. Going to bars.*

When I say "going to bars," I mean the lifestyle that accompanies going to bars all the time. Bars are associated with random hookups, people getting drunk, overindulgence, and lots of other things that aren't good for you.

So, I don't go out to bars anymore. In the nine years Brent and I have been married, we've been to a bar only a couple of times. If you make a list of all the habits that will improve your life, none of those things happen in bars.

*3. Junk food.*

This is a tough one because I love me some Oreos! It's gotten to the point where I can't have them in the house. If they're in the house, then we'll end up making Oreo shakes, or at the very least, consuming more of them than is healthy. (And let's face it . . . there is nothing healthy about Oreos even though they taste amazing.)

If you only have a couple of them, you'll crave more because that is what junk food is designed to do. If you cut out sugar for a week or two, you will stop craving it.

I also don't eat at places like McDonald's. Even if Savannah gets food from there (which is rare), I'll go somewhere else to get something healthier.

*4. Time wasters.*

The biggest excuse people have for not getting healthy is that they don't have time. But nobody has the time. You *make* the time. We all have the same twenty-four hours in a day.

I don't have cable, I rarely watch TV, I don't party, and I don't go to bars. When you cut out all the things that take up so much of an average person's time, you have lots of time for your health. It's simply a matter of making choices to live a healthier lifestyle.

*5. Bad habits.*

There is an endless number of bad habits that hold people back. One of mine was smoking.

I was fourteen years old when I started smoking, and I quit three-and-half years ago. As I mentioned at the beginning of this chapter, I quit because I was afraid it would prevent me from getting into the best shape possible for a body-building competition.

My coach said, "Why would you want to quit smoking

right now?" The reason was that I didn't want it to hold me back. He told me that smoking helps me get more cut. Even so, I quit because it was the last thing that had control over me.

Quitting smoking was the hardest thing I've ever done in my life. I enjoyed having a cigarette with my coffee. It relaxed my mind. If I felt stressed, I would smoke a cigarette.

But I was tired of the smell and tired of being judged. I was tired of it controlling me when I walked out of the house. When I got edgy and uncomfortable during a movie, I'd get up because I needed a cigarette. I couldn't remember a time in my life that I didn't smoke so, I couldn't remember what it was like not to be a smoker.

It was scary, heading into the unknown. But once I got that nicotine out of my system, it was the most freeing feeling in the world. I felt like a new human being!

You have bad habits that are holding you back as well. I want you to know that you can do it. You have the strength to change and become a better version of yourself. Don't underestimate your ability to become something better than you are right now at this moment.

*6. Putting yourself last.*

So many people put themselves at the lowest priority in their life. They let everyone else's needs come first. Do you struggle with this?

Remember, you are worth it! Take the time to make yourself the priority. You'll be a better parent, friend, co-worker, sibling, and boss. Not to mention, you'll be around a lot longer to enjoy the ones you love.

You shouldn't feel guilty about taking time to exercise and get healthy. The best way to show that you love others is to be the healthiest, most energetic version of yourself possible.

*7. Excuses.*

A big problem that I see from parents is that their kids become excuses for not getting healthy. When you have kids, especially younger ones, your life is chaotic, and it's easy to use every excuse in the book for not eating healthy and working out.

But at the end of the day, it's all a choice. If something is important to you, you'll make time for it.

It doesn't take that long to exercise. How many times do we sit and watch an hour of Netflix or YouTube? How many times do we sit and scroll mindlessly on our phones throughout the day? It's very common. But if you were to work out for one hour a few times a week, it would change your whole life. Even if it's just thirty minutes, that's a fantastic start. Everybody has thirty minutes a day.

I'm not immune to this. It's easy to get lost in Facebook land. I can't tell you how I get swallowed down this hole, and I'll be on there an hour and not get one ounce of work done. Then I realize that I've wasted a whole hour doing absolutely nothing because I wasn't focused.

You can easily do thirty minutes of some type of activity each day . . . if you let go of the excuses. One of the best ways to do this is to have a specific goal, like training for a race. When I'm training for a marathon, I'm very focused. I make it a priority because I'm reaching for a goal. Nothing will stop me from that goal! I'll get up at 5:00 a.m. to get my miles in or whatever I need to do.

Anything is possible if you set your mind to it!

## HOW TO GET STARTED

Now we come to the part of the chapter where I finally give you some practical steps. It only took a couple thousand words to get here!

But seriously, I started with all that other stuff because your mindset and attitude are the missing links. If you don't have the right mindset, you'll give up and revert to your bad habits. And trust me, that's a place you don't want to be.

So, where do you begin? How do you get started with getting healthier? I have a few simple suggestions if this is an area that's new to you. If you already work out, if you're already eating healthy, I encourage you to keep on keeping on!

But if you need a good place to begin, here are a few things I recommend:

*1. Get a good pair of running shoes.*

That is priority #1. So many people miss this step. If you don't have decent shoes, you put yourself at risk for injury. Go to a store specializing in running shoes, get measured, so you have a good fit, and then most importantly . . . start using them!

Fair warning; good shoes will set you back a little bit. Be prepared to invest at least $100 in a good pair. In the grand scheme of things, this is a very small amount because the return on your investment will be incalculable.

*2. Start walking.*

I would start by waking up at a decent time to start walking outside. You don't need to start training for a big marathon or anything like that, at least not yet. While you're walking, listen to something that motivates you. (Check out some of the books I mentioned in Chapter 3.)

Just start walking and increase it a little bit at a time. Then incorporate jogging into your walking. When you're out walking, pick a spot and then jog to that spot. Focus on small victories until the battlefield changes. And if you have a dog, you already have a built-in reason for walking more.

This morning, I intended to walk two miles. But when I got to mile two, I forgot where I was because I was so ingrained in the audiobook I was listening to. The awesome thing about walking and listening to audiobooks is that you get all the benefits of exercise, plus all the benefits of reading.

*3. Gradually improve your nutrition.*

When you want to make a positive change in your life, it's tempting to want to change everything at once. But I don't recommend doing that. Good nutrition is essential, but I would not try to cut out all bad foods at once. That is a recipe for failure.

Instead, gradually cut out bad foods and incorporate more good ones like fruits and vegetables. At the same time, increase your water intake each week until you are at a healthy level. Focus on taking those baby steps.

*4. Make a dream board.*

What is your goal with your health? Where do you see yourself in five years? What kind of life do you want to live? Write down the answers to those questions and post them where you can see them every day (like on your bathroom mirror or refrigerator).

The simple act of writing things down by hand is very powerful. There is an intimate connection between your brain and your hand. You don't need to have all the answers to these questions written in excruciating detail. All you need is a dream to keep you moving forward.

*5. Track your time.*

This is a fun exercise that will surprise you. For a two weeks, write down everything you do in fifteen-minute increments. At the end of two weeks, add up how much time you spent on various activities: watching TV, working out, playing with your kids, reading, sleeping, working, etc.

Here's what most people discover. They are spending much less time on important things than they think. Likewise, they are wasting more time than they think on mindless activities. Try this, and you will quickly see where you are wasting time.

*6. Shop smart.*

Here's a dirty little secret of grocery stores: all the healthy food is on the borders of the store. That is where the produce, dairy, and meats are displayed. All the processed food is contained in the aisles.

If you want to make the most of your grocery store visit, shop in a square. It's an easy way to plan your grocery shopping and avoid most of the unhealthy food.

*7. Sleep well.*

There's almost nothing more important than being consistent in your sleep. If you're not a consistent sleeper or consistent in your hours, your body will struggle to lose weight. You'll feel stressed out. When you don't have enough sleep, you'll be angry or experience other symptoms that may be harmful to your health. If you're angry enough, you will also endanger someone else's health!

In his classic book, *The 7 Habits of Highly Effective People*, Stephen Covey talks about Quadrant 2 activities, which are important but not urgent. That is the category where most people put health-related activities.

Getting healthy doesn't seem urgent . . . until it is. Don't wait until life throws you into a tailspin by giving you a heart attack or something worse. Getting healthy and taking care of your body is a great investment of time and energy that will pay massive dividends in every area of your life.

## UNLOCK THE POSSIBILITIES

To improve your health:

1. Write down all the benefits of getting healthy you can think of. What could your life look like in six months, one year, or five years if you made your health a priority?

2. What do you need to sacrifice or give up to be healthier? A bad habit? Junk food? Time? Putting yourself last? Review the list I included earlier and identify the single biggest obstacle keeping you from better health.

What is the single action you could do in the next seven days to get you moving in the right direction?

3. If you don't already exercise, start by walking five minutes, and increase it by five minutes every day for one week. By the end of a week, you'll be walking for over thirty minutes per day!

## 9. LIVE DEBT-FREE

The most famous magician of the 1980s was David Copperfield. He was known for tricks like making the Statue of Liberty disappear and walking through the Great Wall of China.

One of the craziest tricks Copperfield performed was going over Niagara Falls. His hands and feet were locked in chains. Then he was secured inside a box that hung from a raft-like structure. The whole thing was set on fire, and a helicopter hoisted it to a location a short distance away from the edge.

The rushing water moved the raft closer to the drop-off while dramatic music played. It looked like David Copperfield wasn't going to make it. Then the raft disappeared from view. A few moments later, another helicopter came into view with Copperfield dangling from a rope and smiling with that smarmy look he's known for.

But of course, there was a trick. There is always a trick with magicians.

If you get online (I'm not going to spoil the trick), you can find out how Copperfield did it. But once you find out, the trick isn't so impressive. That's why they call it an *illusion*. What you're seeing is not real.

David Copperfield wasn't really locked up in chains. He could escape at any time. He was never in any real danger.

I wish I could say the same for the millions of American families who are deep in debt. They are locked in the chains of debt and cannot escape. The danger to their family and their future is more real than they can possibly imagine. The longer they keep living in debt, the closer they inch toward disaster.

I've been in deep debt more than once. I've already described the terrible situation my ex-husband left me in when he decided to leave. After I was remarried, we found ourselves in debt again. We owed nearly $75,000, but it wasn't due to extravagant living. It was due to ordinary expenses such as school, cars, and a small credit card debt.

We started paying off the debt, and I remember the feeling of getting rid of that $10,000 on the credit card. It was the most freeing feeling to know that I didn't owe anybody anything. We lived on an Air Force base since Brent is in the military, so we didn't have a mortgage.

There is so much freedom in being debt-free. It's the

best freedom you can feel! It's not easy to do, but it's worth it.

Most Americans accept debt as normal. They believe you should get used to it. We are all taught that a mortgage, car payments, student loans, and credit card debt are normal.

We have worked hard to pay off a large amount of debt. Now we are debt-free except for the house. In this chapter, I want to show you how we did it. Even more importantly, I want to inspire you to take action and get rid of the debt that is holding you back.

These days, no one gets thrown into prison for being in debt. You can be sued, you can lose your car and house, and you can go bankrupt. But in the United States, you aren't thrown into an actual prison when you owe money to someone.

The people in Victorian-era Western Europe were not so lucky. If they owed money, they could be locked up in a debtor's prison where they would work until the debt was paid. You may not be locked up in an actual prison, but being in debt sure feels like you are!

If debt is a dream-killer, why are most people content to stay locked up in its chains?

## A PRISON OF OUR OWN MAKING

As I think about my journey of financial mishaps (including temporary bankruptcy after my first husband left) and look at the broader culture, I see four reasons why people get into debt and usually stay there.

First, it's normalized behavior. Almost everyone borrows money for a house, cars, college, and furniture, among other things. The craziest thing I've ever heard of is borrowing money for vacation!

When a behavior is normalized, there is no shame or embarrassment attached to it. I'm not saying that you should feel embarrassed because you are in debt. But just a few decades ago, it was not normal to borrow money for so many things. When our grandparents were growing up, they did not usually borrow money. They saved money and only made a purchase when they had the funds.

Second, we get caught in a comparison trap. Some people call this "keeping up with the Joneses." (Why does the Jones family always get blamed?) If our neighbor gets a new lawnmower or pool, we have to get one as well.

Social media has made the comparison much worse. We see other people's pictures of vacations or their new car, and we want to have those things. It would be a fascinating study to see if the average amount of consumer debt has risen alongside the use of social media in the last ten to fifteen years.

Third, people are seeking happiness through material things. When you're never content with what you have, you go out and try to purchase happiness with more material goods.

Some call this "retail therapy." But shopping your way into a better mood never works because the happiness only lasts a day or two. Buying more things only masks the real problem, which is a lack of contentment.

When you put these three things together, it's a vicious cycle of financial and emotional imprisonment. You have a situation where it's normal to compare yourself to others, feel unhappy, then try to buy happiness by going into more debt.

There's a fourth reason people get into problems with debt, but this one is beyond your control. Sometimes other people's behavior creates financial issues, and you have to deal with them.

Money was a significant source of stress in my first marriage. My ex-husband and I had very different expectations of what should happen with our money. I felt it should go toward bills (like any responsible person would do!). If he came into some extra cash, he would splurge on something fun, even if we had bills to pay. That caused a lot of pain and resentment in our relationship.

When he left, I was saddled with his credit card debt and a mortgage, with only my income to pay for it. He made more money than I did, so you can see why this was a problem. He stopped paying the house and car payments. He simply refused to pay for them anymore. My car was repossessed, and I tried to declare bankruptcy but didn't meet the qualifications.

But over time, I dug my way out. Whatever your situation, know that you can dig your way out, too. Most people don't have the situation I did—someone leaving you with a pile of debt and financial problems. Most of the time, debt is a prison of our making, but sometimes you are locked up in financial prison because of someone else's crimes.

Regardless of how you got into debt, you can get out. I have a few suggestions from personal experience that will help you start making progress.

## 10 PRACTICAL SUGGESTIONS

This is not a complete list of how to handle your finances. Instead, these are ten simple suggestions for getting out of debt and staying that way. If you want a complete system, I recommend checking out books and resources by Dave Ramsey and other financial teachers. In this section, I simply want to share what has worked for us.

One more thing before I dive in. Notice that I said these were simple, not easy. A thing can be very simple yet still very difficult. That's what getting out of debt is like. It's a very straightforward process, but if it were easy, everyone would be doing it, which brings me to the very first point.

*1. Begin with the right attitude.*

If you start the journey toward a debt-free life with a bad attitude, you are doomed from the start.

Your attitude is like the rudder of your life. It will determine your direction. It's more important than your salary, opportunities, or any other external situation. Getting out of debt is, first and foremost, an *inside job*.

You must have a positive attitude that says, "I can do this!" You must embrace this journey because the lessons you learn will apply to other areas of your life. When you get out of debt, you become stronger.

Henry Ford said, "Whether you think you can or think you can't, you're right." Your attitude is the most important part of this whole process.

*2. Buy only the groceries you need.*

When you go to the store to buy groceries, make a list beforehand and only buy what is on that list. If you go to the store when you're bored or hungry and don't have a list, you will buy things you don't need. You'll waste money and put yourself further behind.

If you struggle with buying things on impulse, it might be better to have your spouse do the grocery shopping. If both of you struggle with this, or you're not married, consider using a grocery delivery service. You will spend a little more for the items plus a delivery fee, but you will save money in the long run since you won't buy anything on impulse.

*3. Cook at home.*

When we needed to cut back on spending, we started cooking more at home instead of eating out. We were spending a lot of money on restaurants—probably as much as we spent on groceries.

Cooking at home doesn't need to be complicated. There are lots of recipe websites, books, and YouTube videos on how to cook at home. The main thing is to plan your meals and ingredients beforehand, then stick to it. If you don't have a plan, you will default to the easiest option, which is usually eating out.

*4. Get organized with a budget.*

The biggest reason our spending gets out of control is that we don't know where our money is going. We get to the third week of the month and realize we have another week left before getting paid again! As the saying goes, "You have too much month left at the end of your money."

You can use an old-fashioned pen and paper, a spreadsheet, or a computer program or app. Choose whatever method works best for you. The point is to have a plan for every dollar you will receive in the coming month. And when you track your spending, you can easily see if you are staying on budget.

When you first start using a budget, it feels like torture, as if someone is stealing your freedom. But the opposite is true. When you use a budget and have an intentional plan for your money, you are gaining freedom. You have been locked up in chains for so long that they don't hurt anymore.

As soon as you start trying to get out of those chains, it hurts for a while. But the more you use a budget, the freer you will get, and the looser those chains will become. And pretty soon, you will feel a sense of freedom you have never felt before because you're making progress.

It's important to know upfront that living on a budget will be uncomfortable for a while. You'll have to make cuts that don't feel good. When you see that you've been eating out twenty times a week, it's a little shocking. But you'll immediately see how much money you can save by only eating out a couple of times a week.

*5. Don't buy the best of everything.*

One of the dangers of comparing yourself to the Joneses is that it's easy to feel like you need the best of everything. But the "best" in any product category is usually the result of good marketing. The highest-priced items are usually not the best value. They just have more bells and whistles that don't always add to the functionality of the product.

For example, Brent was going to buy a new hunting bow recently. He looked at many different brands, including the top-of-the-line models.

But then he considered, "What do I really need at this point? If I get a mid-level bow and shoot it for five years, maybe I can upgrade then." If he uses it for five years, he would feel justified in upgrading.

But many times, people buy the best of everything for no reason. You can usually get away with a pair of $30 shoes or a $5 pair of socks. There are exceptions, of course (like buying good running shoes), but in most areas of life, you don't need the very best.

*6. Be honest: do you really need it?*

Americans are so used to living on credit cards that saying "no" to yourself almost feels like punishment. But when you ask yourself whether you really need a certain thing, you begin to feel a sense of freedom. Material objects will not have the control of you they once did.

For example, we have talked about upgrading Brent's truck, but he is okay with sticking with what he's got for now. A new truck would be nice, but he would rather use the money somewhere else or save it for another more important expense.

When you feel tempted to buy that new shiny object, ask yourself whether that is the best use of your money. After all, we are all stewards of what God has given us. The purchase might feel good at the moment, but the feeling will be short-lived. It's helpful to think more long-term.

*7. Make bigger debt payments.*

When you cut back on non-essential spending, what do you do with that extra money? You can put it toward payments that decrease your debt and help you get to freedom faster.

Whenever I got a tax refund, I knew that money would pay down debt faster. That is the value of having a budget—you know where your money is going, and you should already have money allocated for your living expenses. When you get extra cash, it can go toward debt.

It's vital that you and your spouse or partner be on the same page about this. A lot of relationship problems are caused by disagreements about money.

*8. Learn how to deal with debt collectors.*

When my first husband left, he filed a total liquidation bankruptcy. The divorce court could not overturn that, so I was stuck with all the debt. I was living in a cheap little run-down house. I had to sell the house or pay off the debt. It was so stressful.

I had my car repossessed. I was in the bathroom doing my hair after work one day, and they came and took it. It was so embarrassing, and the guys were loud. They were doing it quickly as if I was going to go outside and do something about it.

I was dealing with eleven companies, and the debt collectors would call about once a month. I couldn't afford to make payment plans with all of them at once. I'd let them know I was making a payment on a particular account and that they should call back in a couple of months.

That went on for a good three years. I was paying off these debts, and it was seriously stressful. But one thing I have learned as I've gotten older is that you can't control everything. There is no reason to get stressed about things that are out of your control. Your level of stress and anxiety will not have any impact on the outcome.

If you are going through this, relax and take a deep breath. Take each day as it comes. Do what you can do and know that you will get to it, but it will take time. It's essential to learn how to cope with stress. In fact, dealing with debt collectors is good practice for dealing with any kind of stress!

Create a plan and stick to it. Focus on one creditor at a time, and don't let them overwhelm you. When you talk to them, let them know you're going to take care of the debt, but you can only do one at a time.

Debt collectors are sneaky. They will try to get you to make crazy agreements, but don't take what they offer you right away. Stand your ground, make a plan, and take it one day at a time.

*9. Start a business to make extra money.*

When you are getting out of debt, being frugal and budgeting your money is critical. But you also need to make extra income. Or as Dave Ramsey says, you need a bigger shovel. The more money you have, the faster you can pay off debt and set yourself up for long-term success.

You can work for yourself, or you can work for someone else. When you work for someone else, you're probably going to get a three percent annual raise and two weeks of vacation. That is the best you can probably hope for.

But if you work for yourself, you can give yourself as much of a raise as you want by increasing your work ethic and creativity. You will have more time and more freedom as you grow your business. You get to decide when and where you work and how much you make.

You don't need to quit your job today and start a business. I recommend starting a business on the side and then building it. Take ten or fifteen hours a week to get started. After a year, you should have a profitable business that lays the groundwork for a full-time career.

Remember, there is no security in any job. The security is in *you*.

I started my business in July 2017, when Brent got orders from the Army to move to Albuquerque, New Mexico. I began my new business that same month. I was close to never trying this entrepreneur thing again since I had failed the first time.

Once we got settled, I dabbled a bit and did pretty well. December 2017 came, and I made a decision to put my head down and put everything I had into my business. In the first month, I made $1,200, the second month $11,000, and the third month I made over $31,000.

My life was forever changed that day in February 2018. I have made checks over three times that $31,000 now. It's mind-blowing what you can build when you are consistent and super focused.

You can live a life you only dreamed of before—success you never thought you would ever experience in real life!

*10. Don't give up.*

When you are working toward a challenging goal, sometimes you will feel like quitting. Debt collectors will call, you'll have money fights with your spouse, you'll get tired, and things won't always go as planned.

We paid off $73,500 in debt (not including the house) by getting serious about it. That amount included school tuition, a credit card, student loans, and two cars. But now, that debt is gone, business is booming, and I'm so glad we did it!

Just like Dory says in *Finding Nemo*, "Just keep swimming . . . just keep swimming." Most people give up. But that's why most people stay in debt. I want you to succeed. So just keep swimming.

## THE COLLEGE QUESTION

One of the biggest financial topics today is the high cost of a college education. I would be remiss if I didn't address it here.

I didn't go to college, so I can't speak to the college experience. But I do know this; I now make multiple six figures with my business without a college degree. You don't need a degree to be successful in business and make a great living.

I'm not against college. It's an excellent choice for those who want to pursue careers that require it, such as medicine or law. But for the majority of people, it's not so clear. For me, the ultimate question is; what is the ROI (return on investment) of your college education? Ultimately, a college education is a product that you have purchased, and you should be able to recoup your investment. Not only that, but it should also pay dividends by getting you a higher-paying job.

But that is not always the case. Many college students never finish their degree or don't go into a degree-related career. And we all know that massive student debt is a real problem.

I encourage parents and students to think long and hard before spending a massive amount of money on a college education. If you decide to go to college, make sure you can pay for it. Don't take out loans. And make sure you clearly understand how your college education is going to benefit your career down the road.

There are other alternatives to a traditional four-year college, such as community college, internships, trade school, starting a business, or going straight into the workforce. You can get many of the benefits of college without the expense.

Many people go to college hoping to find a pathway for their life. But that is an expensive experiment! Before you go to college, get clear on your goals and make sure you can pay for it. It might take longer, but it will save you the burden of student debt later on.

## DO YOU WANT FREEDOM?

The question of getting out of debt ultimately comes down to this; how badly do you want freedom? How much do you want to bless your family in future generations? What kind of life do you want for yourself and your kids?

We search for joy and happiness in so many material things. But true joy can't be found in things. It's found in the decision to live life every day, to appreciate and love the ones closest to you, to tackle the challenges you're facing head-on, and to come out on the other side a better, stronger person.

That's exactly who you'll be when you decide to live debt-free once and for all. There will no tricks, no burning rafts, and no going over the edge of Niagara Falls. There will only be peaceful waters where you can rest easy knowing you have created a better future for you and your family.

## UNLOCK THE POSSIBILITIES

To begin moving toward a debt-free life:

1. When you scroll through social media, do you compare yourself to others taking vacations or buying nicer things than you have? If this is a problem, consider doing a "social media fast" or unfollowing anyone who sparks a feeling of jealousy or "comparison-itis."

2. Review the list of ten practical suggestions I've included for getting out of debt. Which three items could you begin doing immediately?

3. If you are married or have a partner, schedule a time to talk about your budget, income, and financial goals. Do your best to get on the same page about money. You will be much stronger working together than working against each other.

## 10. GIVE GENEROUSLY

My dad saved my life, then lost his own six months later.

I've already told you the story of my first husband, who left us with a pile of debt. Because of that situation, I lost my car and was about to lose my house. But my dad is the reason I was able to keep it. He took out a loan on his house, bought mine, and I made the payments through him.

I never asked my dad for anything. I think he believed we were rich because I worked at a cancer center, and my ex-husband worked for the railroad, which is funny because we were definitely not rich.

When everything fell apart, my dad saw the situation and knew I had given it my all. I never asked for anything, so he was willing to do this for me. My dad is the reason my daughter was able to go to a private school. I wouldn't have been able to put money towards that if he had not helped me. He saved my life; then we lost him six months later.

My relationship with my dad was not always good, but I have never forgotten what he did for my daughter and me. I have tried to live in a way that I could help and bless others in the same way that I have been blessed.

That is the culmination of this whole book. Yes, "anything is possible," but what is it all for? It's not just so we can enjoy the blessings and benefits of being healthy, having a purpose, and making more income. There is something much greater.

I remember running on the treadmill one day, listening to Pastor Craig Groeschel from LifeChurch. He was talking about how people with money can be incredibly unhappy. I thought that was a profound insight. It goes against popular logic, which says material things and outward success make you happy. Turns out, they don't. That happiness is a short-lived rush that always leaves you wanting more.

We aren't put on this earth to be selfish and focus on ourselves. What has made me happy is knowing that I'm here to help God's people. My passion in life has gone from what I thought were my goals and purpose to something more than myself. I feel the freest when I'm helping other people change their lives.

That is the true definition of freedom—being able to help another person change their life and live their dream. That is my purpose. That is what I live for.

Money is the great amplifier. If you give someone a lot

of money, it will show you who they truly are. If they had problems before money, it will usually make the problems bigger. But if they were a generous person before, it will help them be even more generous.

I want to teach you a few ways you can give to others and be more generous. But first, we need to talk about the foundation of giving—your mindset.

## THE MINDSET OF GIVING

A mindset is literally how you set your mind. What is your mindset when it comes to being generous?

There are two kinds of people—ponds and rivers. A pond is a collection point for water. Water from a stream or a rainfall can flow in, but it won't flow out. A pond is stagnant, and it sometimes forms "pond scum" on top of the water because it hasn't been refreshed.

A river, on the other hand, is constantly flowing. You can never step into the same river twice because the water is continuously in motion. A river is simply a channel that carries water from one point to another.

Just like a stagnant pond, some people keep everything for themselves. As a result, they become stagnant. Why do they act this way? Because they have a scarcity mindset. They believe there is only so much to go around, so they must hang onto everything they can get. They perceive everyone is out to get them, and they don't want to share.

And just like a flowing river, some people are a never-ending supply of goodness for those around them. They have a mindset of abundance because they know there is more than enough to go around. When they give to people and help others in need, they know it comes back to them in surprising ways.

These people know that giving is fun. It releases the grip of materialism in their lives. They also know they can never "own" anything because it all belongs to God anyway.

The Bible teaches that we are stewards of God's gifts. Some people are uncomfortable with that idea. They don't like the idea that they worked for their money, but God still owns it. But this idea of stewardship—being a manager of someone else's resources—is one of the most freeing ideas you will ever hear. When you understand that none of it belongs to you anyway, you are free to give and receive.

When you die, what happens to your money and possessions? It gets distributed to other people. (Hopefully, it goes to your family if you have taken the proper legal steps.) You can't take it with you when you die, so why hold so tightly to it while you're living?

I didn't always think this way. It took time for me to develop this mindset. Generosity is like a muscle. You have to exercise it to get stronger.

## IS GENEROSITY SELFISH?

This may seem like a weird question, but it's worth asking: If being generous makes us feel good and bring so much positive energy into our lives, is it ultimately a selfish act?

It's hard to talk about generosity and not sound selfish. It's not as if you are doing something for others so that you can get a benefit. Maybe you're giving a free training session to help someone get back on track or doing a live video to make people feel good. There are many ways to give value to people. But the reality is, when you help others, you improve yourself.

One reason that happens is because of the positive vibes that giving brings into your life. When you focus on the positive, more positive things happen. Whatever you focus on gets bigger. It's not that the world around you has changed. The same negative things are happening. But your mindset has changed, so you perceive things in a differently.

I'm not saying you are wearing rose-colored glasses and don't see the negative. It's still there. But you have a different perspective on it. The negative doesn't matter as much.

When you give, it makes you feel good, helps other people, and creates an overall positive atmosphere. Does that make it selfish? It's hard to answer. I'm not sure we ever do anything from a purely selfless motive. But the fact remains that when you give, you do receive something back, even if it's just the knowledge that you helped another person.

## PRACTICAL IDEAS FOR BEING MORE GENEROUS

Generosity is a big topic. I don't want to give you the idea that we have it all figured out. We are just trying to be obedient to God and generous with the blessings He has given us. That said, I want to share a few practical ideas that have guided us in our giving.

I can sum up all my thoughts about giving like this; *You should help someone if you're in a position to do so.*

Don't get me wrong. I'm not a socialist. I'm just saying that if you can help someone, you should. That is what it means to be a good, decent person. And if you call yourself a Christian, it's especially your responsibility, since that is how Jesus lived.

Is there money you can give? If they are sick, can you send food? Do they need a ride or a job reference? You can help in a million ways.

When you help others, it always comes back to you in some way. It's important to give back. We're here for a bigger purpose. We are here to help God's people. That is part of being selfless and giving back to the world.

You can't put a dollar sign on it because you can change somebody's life when you give. That is a priceless reward. But it's not only about giving money or possessions. You can give of yourself. I would rather have somebody give me their time and energy than give me money. There are so many ways to help.

I do my best to give to others who are not as fortunate as me. I donate to people every single month in some way. It might be taking care of their household goods for the month or giving away free meal plans or workout plans because I know their money is tight.

There is probably not a month that goes by where I'm not giving something to help somebody. It makes me feel better, but I'm not doing it to feel better—that's the result. I believe I'm put here to do things like that. And I think that's why God has blessed me the way he has.

I don't plan out my giving. I just pay attention to whatever needs present themselves. I would almost rather help people individually than always give to big organizations. For example, because of COVID, I donated $200 to my friend's restaurant in St. Louis. I said, "Take the money for the people supporting you. Give them a free appetizer on me." It was a way to say thank you to her customers and help a friend with her business.

Being generous and giving is not always about doing big things. Sometimes it's small acts like that that mean the most, especially when helping people directly. It can even be as simple as paying for another person's meal when you go out to eat.

When we go out with others, we almost always pay. We want people to go out and enjoy themselves, experience life, and not have to worry about the bill.

Here's what's funny: I don't have many people in my circle I could call for help, or who are overly generous. But if somebody called me, I'd be quick to help them do something. I have always been that way because I remember not having anything or anybody. I don't ever want to be the person who doesn't help. I always want to be there to help somebody out if I have the means.

I also don't ever want our girls to feel they have to struggle. I don't want them to feel like they are missing out because we don't have the money. There is a balance. You don't want to give your kids everything because it will spoil them. But you do want your kids to feel secure and not worry.

## GIVING WHEN YOU'RE STRUGGLING

If you are struggling financially or trying to work your way out of debt, you might be wondering how you can give to others.

Giving money is only one way to be generous. For example, one of my girlfriends needed help landscaping her yard. I love landscaping, so I went and helped for two days. I didn't need any money to lend a helping hand. You can also have people over for dinner, be a good listener, and simply be a caring friend. There are countless ways to help.

My network marketing business impacts a lot of people, and I'm very active on social media. People often reach out to me with various needs, and sometimes it's the most random thing. I try to listen to them and share my story. I don't make any money from that. I'm lending my ear and giving advice when it's needed.

People's #1 emotional need is to feel loved and affirmed. Many people feel like they have no friends. The simple act of listening compassionately is one of the best ways you can be generous.

## WHAT IF MY SPOUSE IS NOT SUPPORTIVE?

I want to tackle a sensitive issue before bringing this chapter to a close. What if you are a generous person, but your spouse is not? How do you navigate this issue in your relationship if they don't support your desire to give?

If you feel this way, please know that I've been there! My ex-husband was like that. And you see where that got us!

I'm not going to pretend it's easy. It's a difficult issue. It's hard to sit them down and explain why giving is important to you. The most important thing is to hope and pray that they love you enough to be okay with your generosity because it's close to your heart.

Maybe your spouse has never seen generosity modeled for them. They may have grown up in a family where the parents did not help others. If they never had a mentor in this area, how would they know what generosity looks like?

You can't change another person's heart. I couldn't change my ex-husband's heart or attitude, as much as I would have liked to. The best thing you can do is to be a good example. When they see the joy and blessings that come into your life because you are generous, they will probably reconsider their approach. Sometimes, it takes many years for a person to change.

I also encourage you to sit down and have a real adult conversation with your spouse. Talk about what's on your mind, why you feel this way, and why it's important for your family. Most married couples can have an honest conversation about something important to them if the relationship is good.

Unfortunately, not every marriage is healthy. Sometimes a person is not willing to listen or communicate. I'm in a healthy relationship, but I've also been in an unhealthy relationship. When things are unhealthy, and you're not working together as a team, there are bigger issues. If this is your situation, I recommend going to a counselor who can help you walk through those dark times.

Marriage is about compromise. You are supposed to be friends who support one another and figure things out together. You won't always get what you want, but you've got to compromise. You may have to pull back on your ideas for being generous and be willing to adjust for a while.

Here's another idea for giving if your spouse is not on board. In the last chapter, we talked about the need for a budget. One of the advantages of a budget is that you can allocate personal money for each of you. You can use these funds however you want. Some people use it for clothing, eating out, buying gifts for people, or other personal things.

If giving is important to you, but your spouse is not supportive, just give out of your personal funds. It will probably not be as much as if you make it a household line item in your budget, but at least it will be a place to start.

## ANYTHING IS POSSIBLE

Speaking of a place to start—that's a great way to wrap up this book. No matter where you are starting from, you can begin writing a brand new ending for your life story.

If you're starting with doubt and confusion . . . embrace your destiny.

If you've lost your confidence . . . believe in yourself.

If you're stuck in a job you hate . . . find your why.

If you're discouraged about your past mistakes . . . learn from your failures.

If you're living day-to-day with no purpose . . . focus on the future.

If you're struggling with stops and starts in your habits . . . be consistent.

If you need to upgrade your relationships . . . choose your friends wisely.

If you don't have enough energy . . . take care of your body.

If you've lost financial freedom . . . live debt-free.

If you want to feel true joy by serving others . . . give generously.

You have so much potential. You can't even begin to fathom the amount of power you have to change yourself and the world around you. I want you to believe in yourself and know you can do this!

Don't wait until tomorrow. You're not promised another day. Today is the only day you have.

One day, hopefully well into the future, you'll take your final breath. In that moment, what will you be thinking about? Will you feel an overwhelming sense of regret that you never did your best? Or will you feel a massive sense of relief that you gave your best effort?

Anything is possible. But one day in the future, the possibilities will come to an end. You only have a limited amount of time on this earth, so make it count.

When you decide to give your best and start working for it, those possibilities and dreams will become a reality right before your very eyes.

## UNLOCK THE POSSIBILITIES

To start giving generously:

1. Do you have a generous mindset? List three generous things you have done for others in the last month. (If you're struggling to come up with three, you may not be as generous as you think!)

2. If you are struggling financially, what is one thing you can do in the next twenty-four hours to help someone in a way that doesn't require money?

3. When you come to the end of your life, what regrets might you face? What can you do in the next year to prevent those regrets?

## ACKNOWLEDGMENTS

This book is not only a labor of love, it's also the result of a community of people who have encouraged and inspired me along the way.

First, I want to thank my husband, Brent, for inspiring me every day. I could have never written this book without his support behind the scenes.

I also want to thank my daughter, Savannah, for giving me the time and space I needed to make all this happen.

Erin Clark has been a mentor and a light who has guided me every step of the way. She's always a phone call away for anything I need. I would not be where I am today without her.

Thank you to Kent Sanders for helping bring my book to life. Thanks also to Terry Stafford for editing the book, Kristi Griffith for the beautiful cover design, and Boy Aaron Photography for the cover photo.

Finally, I want to thank God because without Him, I wouldn't be here today. He gave me the strength to overcome the obstacles that stood in my way. He is the Almighty reason that every last bit of this has been possible.

## ABOUT THE AUTHOR

Sadie Kolves is a successful entrepreneur who loves to help others become stronger and more confident. She grew up in a small Midwestern town where she learned to overcome setbacks by working hard and believing in herself. Sadie discovered a passion for network marketing and grew it into a multiple six-figure business in just a few years.

Whether it's finishing a marathon, walking across a stage for a bodybuilding competition, or helping people change their lives, Sadie's goal is to achieve more and reach higher. She loves her workouts, her coffee, and, most of all, her family. You can find out more about Sadie at SadieKolves.com.